W9-BGP-391

BROOKLYN

BAY RIDGE
1. Robicelli's Bakery

BEDFORD-STUYVESANT
2. Brooklyn Delhi
3. Brooklyn Soda Works
4. Cracked Candy
5. Doc's All Natural Spirits
6. Fatty Sundays
7. J. W. Overbey & Co.
8. KBBK
9. Krumville Bake Shop
10. Mama O's Premium Kimchi
11. Monsieur Singh
12. People's Pops
13. Rawpothecary
14. Salt of the Earth Bakery
15. SCRATCHbread
16. Sfoglini
17. Spoonable
18. Sweet Deliverance

BENSONHURST
19. Queen Ann Ravioli & Macaroni

BOERUM HILL
20. Nunu Chocolates

BROOKLYN NAVY YARD
21. Kings County Distillery

BROWNSVILLE
22. Fox's U-Bet

BUSHWICK
23. Fine & Raw

CANARSIE
24. Ba-Tampte

CARROLL GARDENS
25. Other Half Brewing Company

CLINTON HILL
26. Dough
27. The Good Batch
28. Salty Road

CROWN HEIGHTS
29. Brooklyn Bell
30. Butter & Scotch
31. Pelzer's Pretzels

DUMBO
32. Brooklyn Roasting Company

EAST WILLIAMSBURG
33. Bacchanal Sauce
34. Brooklyn Hemispherical Bitters
35. Joyva
36. The Noble Experiment
37. OMilk

FORT GREENE
38. Sunny Bang Private Label

GOWANUS
39. Ample Hills Creamery
40. Brooklyn Brine
41. Gotham Greens

GREENPOINT
42. Acme Smoked Fish
43. Anarchy in a Jar
44. Bellocq Tea Atelier
45. Café Grumpy
46. Grady's Cold Brew
47. Greenhook Ginsmiths
48. Greenpoint Trading Company
49. Mombucha
50. New York Distilling Company
51. Ovenly
52. P & H Soda Company
53. Pie Corps
54. Van Leeuwen Artisan Ice Cream

PARK SLOPE
55. Bagel Hole
56. Bark Hot Dogs
57. The Brooklyn Biscuit Company
58. Gorilla Coffee
59. Miti Miti
60. Queen Majesty
61. Union St. Honey

PROSPECT HEIGHTS
62. Cecil & Merl
63. Empire Mayonnaise Co.
64. The Kale Factory

RED HOOK
65. BAKED
66. Cacao Prieto
67. Early Bird Foods & Co.

68. Jack from Brooklyn
69. La Newyorkina
70. Raaka
71. Red Hook Winery
72. Salvatore Bklyn
73. Six Point Brewery
74. Steve's Authentic Key Lime Pies
75. Tin Mustard
76. Uncouth Vermouth
77. Van Brunt Stillhouse
78. The White Moustache
79. Widow Jane

SHEEPSHEAD BAY
80. Jomart Chocolates
81. Michael's of Brooklyn

SUNSET PARK
82. Barrow's Intense
83. Bien Cuit
84. Blue Marble
85. Colson Patisserie
86. Gillies Coffee Company
87. Granola Lab
88. Hana Pastries
89. Industry City Distillery
90. Jacques Torres Chocolate
91. Liddabit Sweets
92. One Girl Cookies
93. Regal Vegan
94. Sahadi's Fine Foods, Inc.
95. Saucy By Nature
96. Sohha Savory Yogurt
97. Tumbador Chocolate
98. Whimsy & Spice

VINEGAR HILL
99. Damascus Bakery

WILLIAMSBURG
100. Brooklyn Brewery
101. Brooklyn Cupcake
102. Brooklyn Wok Shop
103. Buena Vista Tortillas
104. Mast Brothers
105. Morris Kitchen
106. Oslo Coffee Roasters

WINDSOR TERRACE
107. Joray Fruit Rolls

SUSANNE KÖNIG & MELISSA SCHREIBER VAUGHAN

PHOTOGRAPHS BY HEATHER WESTON

MADE in BrOOklyn

AN ESSENTIAL GUIDE TO THE BOROUGH'S ARTISANAL FOOD & DRINK MAKERS

pH powerHouse Books Brooklyn, NY

MADE in Brooklyn

AN ESSENTIAL GUIDE TO THE BOROUGH'S ARTISANAL FOOD & DRINK MAKERS

Text © 2015 Susanne König
Text © 2015 Melissa Schreiber Vaughan
Photographs © 2015 Heather Weston

Photo Credits:
Bien Cuit—Portrait and seeds in hands: Scott Brownlee
All others: Brian Kennedy
Bark Hot Dogs—Right page: Evan Sung
Gotham Greens—Right page, upper left with clam
shells; middle image: Mark Weinberg
Hana Pastries—Blueberry muffin: Justin N. Lane
Six Point Brewery—Maker portrait: Michael Harlan Turkell
Van Leeuwen Artisan Ice Cream—Right side, top image with truck;
ice cream cartons; chef with sugar: Sidney Bensimon
Red Hook—Krzysztof Poluchowicz
Heather Weston author portrait: Errolyn Daley
Melissa Schreiber Vaughan author portrait: Daniel Paterna

All rights reserved. No part of this book may be reproduced in any
manner in any media, or transmitted by any means whatsoever,
electronic or mechanical (including photocopy, film or video recording,
Internet posting, or any other information storage and retrieval system),
without the prior written permission of the publisher.

Published in the United States by powerHouse Books,
a division of powerHouse Cultural Entertainment, Inc.
37 Main Street, Brooklyn, NY 11201-1021
telephone 212.604.9074, fax 212.366.5247
e-mail: info@powerHouseBooks.com
website: www.powerHouseBooks.com

First edition, 2015

Library of Congress Control Number: 2015946181

Hardcover ISBN 978-1-57687-760-9

Printed by Toppan Leefung

Book design by Krzysztof Poluchowicz

10 9 8 7 6 5 4 3 2 1

Printed and bound in China

GREEN
CROWN HE
CAN
BAY
D
EAST WILLIAMS
RED
FORT GI
BENSON
BROOKLYN NAVY
CARROLL GAF
CLINTO
PARK
BOERU
SUNSET
PROSPECT HE
BEDFORD- STUYV
BUSH
VINEGA
GOW
BROWN
WILLIAMS
SHEEPSHEA
WINDSOR TE

CONTENTS

FOREWORD

SWEET FOODS · SAVORY FOODS · COFFEE, TEA BEVERAGES · ALCOHOLIC DRINKS

I'm a New Yorker. I grew up in Queens and went to culinary school in Manhattan. Immersed in culinary culture and working as a recipe developer, I knew my way around the Manhattan food scene. But when I moved to Park Slope in the spring of 2002, all my hard-won knowledge of that scene went out the window. It was almost like I'd moved to a completely new town. Although I'd been to a few of Brooklyn's vanguard restaurants, like Cucina, al di la, and Chickenbone Café, I knew little about local food producers.

Almost immediately some foodie friends told me about a guy named Steve Tarpin who was making key lime pies from scratch in an industrial warehouse on Pier 41 in Red Hook. Mostly he sold wholesale to restaurants, but my friends told me that Steve would happily sell a pie to anyone who happened to catch him in the bakery. When I decided to host my first rooftop party in June 2002, I knew I had to track down and serve Steve's key lime pies. I had never been to Red Hook before, but I wasn't going to let that stop me. I drove over, nervously navigating the cobblestone streets and abandoned lots, until I found a distinctive yellow door hand painted with the words, "Pies Here." I walked into the kitchen and, luckily, Steve was there. I bought my first Brooklyn-made artisanal product directly from the artisan. The setting was gritty and urban, but the moment (and the pie) sweet and satisfying.

Jump ahead to 2009. The dining scene in Brooklyn is flourishing and I'm working on a cookbook with recipes and stories from 31 of the new restaurants that "Put Brooklyn on the Culinary Map." My photographer, Michael Harlan Turkell, suggests we look at some of the rising stars of Brooklyn's artisanal food scene. That's when I first meet folks like Betsy Devine (Salvatore Bklyn), Nekisia Davis (Early Bird), Kheedim Oh (Mama O's), and Rick and Michael Mast (Mast Brothers). Inadvertently,

I'd stumbled upon the front line of Brooklyn's first wave of high-profile DIY innovators. Over the next five years, I watched this fertile creative landscape flourish from a front row seat.

Susanne approached me in the summer of 2014 with the idea of collaborating on a book celebrating the local artisanal food and drinks movement. As a Dumbo-based bookseller and purveyor of locally handmade goods, Susanne has a unique perspective on the scene. She is a well-seasoned cultural attaché for Brooklyn, and I jumped at the opportunity to work with her, meet the makers, and share their stories. We set out with our intrepid photographer, Heather Weston, to capture the essence and diversity of the makers and the ethos of the artisan community—and of course, to taste everything we could get our hands on.

In the process, we met makers whose families had established food businesses long before the current small-batch scene took hold. In the shadow of giants like Domino Sugar and the Brooklyn Navy Yard, small producers smoked fish and roasted coffee, hand rolled pasta, and hand dipped chocolates. They worked long hours to provide for their families and, in turn, nurtured their communities through the common language of food.

More recently, a new wave of artisanal makers arrived on the scene ready to reimagine the culinary landscape and weave new ideas into the existing fabric. Just as hardworking as those who came before, today's makers strive for authenticity and precision. That's not to say they don't understand the value and power of social media. Word spreads so fast, it's often hard to meet the demand (much thanks in part to Brooklyn's brand ambassadors Gaia DiLoreto, owner of By Brooklyn, and Eric Demby and Jonathan Butler, founders of The Brooklyn Flea, Smorgasburg, and Berg'n, all profiled in this book). But still, they stay true to the core values of small-batch artisanal production.

Now it's time for our readers to dive in. Consider this a sourcebook, travel guide, and coffeetable book all in one. We start with a look back in two essays from *Edible Brooklyn* contributing editor Rachel Wharton, a renowned food journalist and expert on Brooklyn's food-making scene, and cocktail historian David Wondrich, the foremost authority on American cocktails. Rachel and David reflect on Brooklyn's history of food production and distilling, framing the recent explosion of artisanal food-and drink-making in the borough.

Profiles of each maker follow and give a taste of who each maker is and why they do what they do. Arranged alphabetically by brand name, along with their stories, each profile page provides the maker's name, the date they established their brand, the product they make, and their web address. Heather's intimate portraits and behind-the-scenes visual reportage of process and product take center stage and are guaranteed to leave you salivating.

Neighborhoods are noted at the top of each page along with four icons, created exclusively for this project. These help let you know at a glance what sort of product you're looking at: Sweet Foods; Savory Foods; Tea, Coffee, Beverages; and Alcoholic Drinks. You'll find two indexes in the back of the book, one by product and one by neighborhood. So if you need a coffee fix, flip to the product index. Or if you're in Greenpoint and want to check out nearby makers, use the neighborhood index. We've included a map of a singular microcosm of the "Made in Brooklyn" food and drink phenomena, Red

Hook, for quick reference and convenient planning. It's a wonderful day trip.

Although we worked on this book for close to ten months, there are many makers we didn't get to visit or photograph simply because there weren't enough hours in the day. We've compiled a list in the back of the book of those we wish we had not missed.

No doubt we are bursting with Brooklyn pride. But we know there are many inspiring and thriving communities of local small-batch artisans beyond Brooklyn's borders. The same DIY energy we thrive on is making a difference and enhancing the local flavor in cities across the globe. In Portland and Oakland, Stockholm and Paris, makers are creative as hell, sharing with the hungry masses and, hopefully, making a living doing what they love.

We hope *Made in Brooklyn* will inspire and guide you to taste new things, maybe even try your hand at making something yourself. Drop us a line when you eat something that blows your mind. Hope to hear from you soon: MadeinBrooklyn@powerHouseBooks.com.

—**Melissa Schreiber Vaughan**, Brooklyn, 2015

INTRODUCTION

PART I: FOOD

You could argue this all began one summer Sunday in 2007, when a couple of friends who worked in the food business decided to host a last-minute expo in the graffiti-tagged backyard of a local dive bar. Gathering a handful of folks they knew who made handcrafted provisions on a small scale or maybe even as a hobby—soft-ripened goat cheese, stone-ground chocolate, pickled pears, rooftop honey—they set up folding tables under the shadow of the Williamsburg Bridge, offering samples for a "suggested donation" of just $5.

Billed as "The Unfancy Food Show," the afternoon was intended as an underground, do-it-yourself antidote to the annual international specialty food fair taking place across the river in Manhattan. A high-stakes trade shindig, it's where big manufacturers go to hawk their crunchy peanut butters or cured Spanish ham to even bigger retail chains in hopes for some space on a supermarket shelf. Back in that Brooklyn bar, on the other hand, some of those Unfancy makers had little more than a hand-stamped logo on a brown paper bag and a plan to talk up their passion to strangers, one jar of pickles at a time. They didn't have marketing managers, distribution chains, or even much Brooklyn brand recognition, back then. But what they did have were great products, the desire to create them on their own terms using the best ingredients, and a growing community of like-minded thinkers.

That would become apparent to the rest of the borough by the next spring, when aspiring Brooklyn makers with zero budget and big dreams scored their first regular marketplace. It was an outdoor bazaar called The Brooklyn Flea (page 196), which took up residence on a high school athletic court once a weekend. For a pittance, a part-time producer could now rent space to put up a table and sell enough of the sour cherry soda they made in a borrowed restaurant kitchen—in the wee hours, after dinner service was over—to finally quit

their day job. Presto: A makeshift incubator for small-batch food products was born.

Eventually, the vendors selling basil and plum popsicles (see People's Pops, page 142), mind-bogglingly rich hand-strained ricotta (see Salvatore Bklyn Ricotta, page 162), and milk chocolate-peanut butter-banana ganache-brown butter cookie candy bars (see Liddabit Sweets, page 110), became as much of a draw as secondhand clothes and vintage furniture. Not only did the founders of the Flea eventually start their own venue just for food (known as Smorgasburg, it boasts 100 vendors feeding 10,000 visitors on Saturdays), they also inspired at least half a dozen similar grassroots markets around the city.

As all these businesses grew, so too did the community—some might call it the infrastructure—supporting them. In the early days, a jam maker might double-up with a baker in the rarely used kitchen behind a friend's specialty food shop, which could then sell their handiwork. Or a soda pop shop would rent out an hour at a commercial or restaurant kitchen. Eventually some grew so big they had to carve out a few yards at a defunct catering operation in an old banana warehouse by Industry City, Brooklyn's industrial waterfront—an area that is now filled with so many businesses the ground floor of one warehouse has been fitted with a swanky cafe and retail shop. Indeed in recent years, both Brooklyn's Navy Yard and a decommissioned pharmaceutical plant on the edge of Bed-Stuy have followed suit to become little cities of food production—hallways bustling with workers packing kimchee or kombucha, sharing sugar, merchandising advice and, more often than not, lunch. And as they all started making sales to national retailers like Whole Foods, West Elm, and Williams-Sonoma (whose buyers made a special trip to Brooklyn to scope out its food makers in 2010), small-scale distributors ferrying their products to and fro blossomed too, yielding a whole group of drivers and deliverers who knew the routes between all of the above by heart.

If this all sounds like serious business, today it is: According to a city-funded study, food products are currently the only growing sector of manufacturing in the Big Apple, and production is concentrated right here in Brooklyn. In 2014 the Brooklyn Chamber of Commerce responded by launching a certified Brooklyn Made label for local manufacturers, nearly half of whom produce food, and started its very own trade show to show them off. The city and state are deeply invested in this process, as well: There are industrial districts, loans and grants, plans for business incubators and updated manufacturing guidelines to help Brooklynites of all stripes start new businesses or lure expanding ones here instead of cities in Oregon, Tennessee, or Texas (see The White Moustache, page 176). Not surprisingly, Brooklyn now has its very own table at that annual professional trade show in Manhattan.

True, it should be noted that the history of cooks coming to Brooklyn to make a start of it is a long one, as is this borough's obsession with its own foodways. One need only ask any Brooklyn resident over the age of 50 about real bagels, Leske's Bakery's black and white cookies, Junior's cheesecake, Ebinger's "Blackout Cake," the red sauce at Michael's of Brooklyn (page 193), or even Lundy Brothers Restaurant's flaky biscuits to get an earful. They maybe even worked at Fox's U-Bet in Brownsville (page 68), or made bonbons with Jomart in Sheepshead Bay (page 94), or worked in one of the thousands more little factories that dotted this borough's once thriving industrial areas.

Yet plenty of cities have both pride of place and the products to back that up. If you're reading this book now, you likely already know that something even bigger is afoot. The newest Brooklyn food makers are generally considered part of an international culinary phenomenon, a best-selling brand (in Paris, these days, they say "très Brooklyn"), and a beacon for creativity and new ideas in producing all kinds of good tasting things.

Indeed, when you ask leaders in the specialty food industry around the country to tell you what a "Brooklyn-made" food product currently means to them, you usually hear statements like these: "The alternative to the expected or the big." "Good quality, a sense of pride, of supporting your local economy, of supporting people you know." "There's not 10,000 of them on a supermarket shelf: it's exclusive, it's small, it has a great story." Or as one expert so eloquently put it: "It's punk rock for food."

If you consider the hallmarks of both genres—back to the technical basics, DIY, anti-establishment—in many ways it's true. In fact, we're pretty sure that's exactly what the folks who planned that first Unfancy Food Show had in mind.

—**Rachel Wharton**, Brooklyn, 2015

INTRODUCTION

PART II: DRINKS

In the summer of 1986, my then-girlfriend Karen and I moved into an old wood-frame row house on the ragged eastern edge of Boerum Hill. The neighborhood was pretty rough. Lots of SRO rooming houses, hookers, crack dealers, decay. On the plus side, if the wind was right, it smelled like fresh-roasted coffee. In the summer, though, and this is definitely on the minus side, if the wind was wrong, it smelled like sour, rotten cheese. There was a reason for each: up on the next block from us was Farinon coffee roasters; down on Bergen Street was the Icco pizza-cheese factory. The old Brooklyn, of which Farinon and Icco were holdouts, had been home to lots of such places.

In fact, old Brooklyn was awash in local drinks. The part of Gowanus that real estate agents would eventually carve off and rename Boerum Hill was known for its coffee roasters. Williamsburg and Bushwick were known for breweries—in 1900, there were at least 45 of them in the city (yes, I know Brooklyn was no longer an independent city after 1898, but it will always be a city, not a borough, to me), with at least a dozen of them in "Brewers' Row," a two-block stretch of Scholes and Meserole Streets in Bushwick. Schaefer and Rheingold were big national brands. (There was even a brewery, and not a micro one, on my block in Boerum Hill: shockingly, most of the physical plant of the Long Island Brewery, as it was known, is still there, although its shipping yard is now a taxi garage and its main building is now occupied by editors and tech workers and such.)

There wasn't a lot of wine made for sale in Brooklyn, although once Italians and Jews from Eastern Europe started flooding into the city in the late nineteenth century a tradition of backyard winemaking took root in some neighborhoods, and kosher winemaking in others. Whiskey and gin were another story, though. The "City of Churches," as Brooklyn was known, had plenty of distilleries, too, many of them centered

around Fulton Landing. In the early years, they ranged in size from the large, and rather noisome, Cunningham & Harris, which was turning out the equivalent of 20,000 bottles of "pure spirits, whiskey gin and brandy" a day (one wonders about that brandy, as they were a grain distillery) and whose system of auctioning off their spent grain to cart drivers often blocked Front Street, to the mom-and-pop Thomas H. Redding & Co., which made 20 kinds of cordials and bitters in a storefront on what's now Old Fulton Street. After the Civil War, the city worked to banish distilling. That effort's success can be judged by the *New York Evening Telegram*'s 1871 claim "every time they put up a new church in Brooklyn, a whiskey distillery is constructed, showing what attention Brooklynites pay to the spirit." Most of those new distilleries were illicit, and raids were frequent. Nonetheless, small, underground distilleries flourished until Prohibition, at which point they became large, underground distilleries. Ironically, Repeal saw the end of the industry as the new licensing laws were onerous and legal whiskey from Kentucky and Pennsylvania and Maryland and such was cheap enough to compete with the illegal stuff on price and easily exceeded it in quality.

Brooklyn's drinks weren't all alcoholic, of course. Seltzer works and other soft-drink companies were scattered throughout the city. One or two of them even made it through to the 1980s: in our early days on Dean Street, Karen and I put away an awful lot of the ironically-named Manhattan Special coffee soda, made in Williamsburg since 1895 and available at every bodega in the neighborhood. But that was pretty much the only Brooklyn-made product we drank. Schaefer and Rheingold, the last two local beers, had gone away in 1976 (and, as I recall from my high school days, weren't so very tasty by then anyway). There certainly were no local whiskeys, gins, or rums. The very idea would have been preposterous; since Repeal, opening a distillery involved such an arduous and expensive legal process that only a dipsomaniac billionaire would chance it.

The 1980s marked the end of a long process of industrial consolidation and homogenization that saw quirky local manufacturers forced to either expand and de-quirk their products or shut down entirely. Once quality or local taste were off the table, products had to compete on price alone, and Brooklyn was just too expensive a location to do business in, in every way—taxes, labor, transportation, construction, you name it. It wasn't just Brooklyn that was affected by this—the sad history of Baltimore Pure Rye, whose 150-year-old tradition was utterly extinguished in the 1950s, is proof of that—but it hit Brooklyn harder than most.

The first sign I saw that the conversation was changing came in the spring of 1988, when my local bodega began stocking a new beer with a big, bold Milton Glaser "B" on the label. Brooklyn Lager actually tasted like something, and it was locally owned (and, soon enough, locally brewed) and we drank it when we could afford it. It cost a little more than the usual domestic beers, but it tasted a lot better. Brooklyn had a strong inferiority complex back then, and here was something that was not only good on its own, it was (we thought) better than Manhattan's New Amsterdam Amber, introduced a few years before. It would prove to be a harbinger of change.

Nonetheless, for quite a while Brooklyn Lager was pretty lonely on the shelf. The late 1980s and early 1990s saw Brooklyn struggling with crack and decay. It wasn't until the mid 90s that things began turning around, and suddenly you saw new restaurants and bars cautiously opening their doors for business. In the fullness of time, these helped to retain the young, creative types who, in decades past, would have stayed in Brooklyn only until they could afford to move to Manhattan. Instead, they took advantage of the then-reasonable commercial rents the city had to offer and began opening interesting things. First came breweries—Red Hook's Sixpoint, which opened in 2004, was a harbinger of this second wave of revival. Then we got the distilleries: changes to New York State liquor laws in 2002 and, more significantly, 2007 made it possible to run a small distillery almost anywhere in the state, as long as you used raw materials grown in-state. In 2010, the Kings County Distillery began making whiskey in tiny batches in East Williamsburg. 2011 saw the New York Distilling Company open, also in Williamsburg, and the innovative Industry City Distillery opened in Sunset Park. The next year—well, they keep opening, to the point that it's hard to keep track of them. Brooklyn even gained a commercial winery, when Red Hook Winery started vinifying back in 2008.

And of course, it's not just alcohol. One day way back in 2002 I was walking down Fifth Avenue near my house and I noticed a new coffee joint, with a glowering red gorilla on its sign. Ten minutes later, jolted to the core, I knew that the neighborhood was back in the coffee game, and how. As with the distilleries, I can't even keep track of all the local coffee roasters and soda-works, not to mention the kombucha-fermenters, bitters-smiths, and what-have-you.

It feels good. Brooklyn used to be a dynamic city of its own, in Manhattan's shadow, but not in its shadow, if you know what I mean. Now, it's back. Hell, with all the big towers flying up downtown, the condos in Williamsburg, the new construction everywhere, that's plain. But that's Manhattanification. It's the small-scale, interesting little businesses that represent the real Brooklyn revival; the rebirth and reinventions of traditions that go back to Dutch times. So bring 'em on!

—David Wondrich, Brooklyn, 2015

ACME SMOKED FISH

YEAR ESTABLISHED: 1954
PRODUCTS: smoked fish
OWNER: Caslow family
WEBSITE: acmesmokedfish.com

I am a devoted consumer of all things Acme Smoked Fish has to offer. Friday mornings roll around and the first thing on my mind is getting to the Gem Street smoked fish plant in Greenpoint for my share of the best smoked salmon, whitefish, and herring I've ever tasted.

The Acme tradition dates back to 1906, when Russian immigrant Harry Brownstein began selling smoked fish from local smokehouses to appetizing stores throughout the city from his horse-drawn wagon. In 1954, Brownstein set up shop with his sons and, four generations later, Acme Smoked Fish is still a family-run business with thousands of wholesale customers nationwide.

A true Brooklyn institution, they've embraced the community around them and have established a tremendous and loyal following as diverse as Brooklyn itself. On Fish Fridays, Acme opens the factory doors to sell direct to the public, for a few precious hours, at wholesale prices. Acme's unwavering commitment to quality and to their Greenpoint neighborhood makes them the elder statesmen of the Brooklyn gastronome community and an inspiration to the smaller food artisans.

—MSV

AMPLE HILLS CREAMERY

YEAR ESTABLISHED: 2011
OWNER: Brian Smith and Jackie Cuscuna
PRODUCT: ice cream
WEBSITE: amplehills.com

The pastoral spirit of old Brooklyn—once verdant farmland complete with grazing cows—was an inspiration for this all-natural, community-aware company, which takes its name from a line in Walt Whitman's classic poem "Crossing Brooklyn Ferry," a meditation on the unity of human experience. And nothing unites us like ice cream! When they opened Ample Hills Creamery, Brian Smith indulged a childhood dream of making his own ice cream and Jackie Cuscuna devised a gathering place where it could be shared and foster the community.

Ample Hill makes its delicious varieties of ice cream entirely from scratch on-site, starting with creating its own base mix by pasteurizing locally sourced milk, then churning it with cream, sugar, and eggs. There are no extracts in Ample Hills' ice cream: flavoring ingredients are sourced directly, steeped in-shop, and slowly added to the mix, drawing exquisite and crazy flavors out of candied bacon, root beer, potato chips, and saltine crackers. Brian also collaborates with fellow makers, including Red Hook's own Sixpoint, whose Righteous Ale he mixed with toffee- and chocolate-covered peanuts to make Righteous Nutz, and Steve's Authentic Key Lime Pies (page 172), chunks of which stud Sunset in the Keys.

Try Ample Hills' signature flavors, including Salted Crack Caramel and Sweet as Honey, at locations in Prospect Heights and Gowanus, or at any one of their three ice cream carts in Brooklyn Bridge Park during summer.

—SK

ANARCHY IN A JAR

YEAR ESTABLISHED: 2009
OWNER: Laena McCarthy
PRODUCT: jam, mustard
WEBSITE: anarchyinajar.com

With a slogan like, "The revolution starts in your mouth," you know Anarchy in a Jar is serious about their preserves. Anarchy's jam queen, Laena McCarthy, started experimenting with jam making in 2009, having learned the craft from her mother while growing up in the Hudson Valley. Laena combines old-world techniques with modern flavors and creates products she describes as "freedom from food tyranny."

Anarchy in a Jar makes more than a dozen varieties of small-batch, shelf-stable jam, chutney, marmalade, and mustard. They're cooked by hand and sustainably produced using fruit and vegetables from small local farms. The simple combination of seasonal fruit, a touch of sugar, botanicals, and spices creates complex, well-melded and not overly sweet delicacies.

Laena credits her peers in the local Brooklyn food-making scene with helping her to thrive and run a successful small business where everyone is learning together. In turn, she is generous and eager to demystify jam making for those who might otherwise be afraid to try it. Through regular updates on her blog, including recipes and tasting suggestions, Laena nurtures a personal and transparent relationship with her customers and her community.

—MSV

BA-TAMPTE

YEAR ESTABLISHED: 1953
OWNER: Silberstein family—Howard, Barry, Seth, and Scott
PRODUCT: pickles, sauerkraut, mustard
WEBSITE: batamptepickles.com

Growing up in Queens, I was surrounded by kosher delicatessens, temples of Jewish soul food that served towering layers of corned beef, pastrami, and brisket, sandwiched between the freshest rye and slathered with bright yellow deli mustard. No deli sandwich was complete without the most perfect sour or half-sour pickle spear on the side. Today, most of these beloved establishments are gone. But Ba-Tampte, a family owned and operated old-school, New York-style pickle producer, is alive and well in Brooklyn, keeping supermarkets and diners nationwide well stocked with pickles (and mustard and sauerkraut, too) that taste like they are fresh from the barrel.

Meyer Silberstein established Ba-Tampte, which means "tasty" in Yiddish, in 1953. He learned the pickle business from his father and grandfather who ran pickle stands and pushcarts on the Lower East Side after emigrating from Romania. Today, Meyer's sons, Howard and Barry, and their sons, Seth and Scott, follow Meyer's original recipe, salt-brining, fermenting, and hand-packaging kirby cucumbers, green tomatoes, and cabbage for sauerkraut in their Brooklyn Terminal Market factory in Canarsie.

Arriving at the factory every morning before 5 AM, the Silbersteins are a hardworking and dedicated bunch, sloshing around in brine and seasonings, kibitzing with their employees, unloading palettes of produce and jars to be hand-packed full of this humble immigrant staple that's still very much in demand today. Ba-Tampte's pickles aren't artisanal in the new sense of the word, but curing cukes as they've always been done—with a fresh garlicky kick and a perfect balance of salt, vinegar, and satisfying crunch—is definitely an art form.

—MSV

BAGEL HOLE

YEAR ESTABLISHED: 1986
OWNER: Phil Romanzi
PRODUCT: old-school bagels

Phil Romanzi of Bagel Hole prides himself on being an old-school bagel maker. He turns out small, crusty, and chewy bagels, freshly boiled and baked daily, which any Brooklyn old-timer can tell you are the real thing. The once ubiquitous traditional-style bagel began to yield to the softer, sweeter, and much larger mass-produced variety in the 1980s, but Phil remains true to the original recipe—each of his bagels is hand-rolled, boiled, and baked in the traditional way.

Phil learned the art of the hand-rolled bagel from a bagel-maker from Sheepshead Bay, whose bagel-making skills had been acquired as a young man in Germany during the 1940s. Phil's next stop was a bagel bakery in Gravesend. Eventually, he was ready to run his own shop, and in 1986, he opened the no-frills, shoebox–sized deli, Bagel Hole, in Brooklyn's South Slope.

Today, Phil still makes all his bagels by hand, following that original recipe, in the same tiny storefront, where he boils and bakes about 12,000 to15,000 rolls a day. At Bagel Hole, you can get bagels in eleven regular flavors, from plain and egg to pumpernickel and salt (no blueberry here!). Try one and see why Bagel Hole is frequently chosen as a purveyor of one of NYC's best bagels by bagel aficionados.

—SK

BAGEL
HOLE

SAVORY
FOODS

PARK
SLOPE

HOT BAGELS
HAND ROLLED   FRESH DAILY

1	1.ᵒᵒ	13	13.ᵒᵒ	25	25.ᵒᵒ
2	2.ᵒᵒ	14	14.ᵒᵒ	26	26.ᵒᵒ
3	3.ᵒᵒ	15	15.ᵒᵒ	27	27.ᵒᵒ
4	4.ᵒᵒ	16	16.ᵒᵒ	28	28.ᵒᵒ
5	5.ᵒᵒ	17	17.ᵒᵒ	29	29.ᵒᵒ
6	6.ᵒᵒ	18	18.ᵒᵒ	30	30.ᵒᵒ
7	7.ᵒᵒ	19	19.ᵒᵒ	31	31.ᵒᵒ
8	8.ᵒᵒ	20	20.ᵒᵒ	32	32.ᵒᵒ
9	9.ᵒᵒ	21	21.ᵒᵒ	33	33.ᵒᵒ
10	10.ᵒᵒ	22	22.ᵒᵒ	34	34.ᵒᵒ
11	11.ᵒᵒ	23	23.ᵒᵒ	35	35.ᵒᵒ
12	12.ᵒᵒ	24	24.ᵒᵒ	36	36.ᵒᵒ

BUY A DOZEN   GET 1 FREE
LOOK FOR OUR SPECIALS
Raisin & Egg   5¢ EXTRA

BAKED

YEAR ESTABLISHED: 2005
OWNER: Matt Lewis and Renato Poliafito
PRODUCT: classic American cookies,
    brownies, cakes
WEBSITE: bakednyc.com

Matt Lewis and Renato Poliafito quit their ad agency day jobs a few months after meeting at work to pursue their lifelong dreams of making cake and coffee. Renato grew up watching and learning while his mother baked; Matt shared his mom's deep love for a good cake mix. Together, they decided that a shared passion for classic American desserts was the perfect impetus to start a new business. Their business plan? A one-line marketing summary: "Open a great American bakery that is not a cupcake shop."

With gumption and wide-eyed naïveté, Matt and Renato opened BAKED in January, 2005, in Red Hook, a neighborhood chosen as much for its cheap rent as for its off-the-beaten track feel. Here they had the room and psychic freedom to experiment with reinterpreting classic American recipes.

BAKED's most popular items are the "Brookster" (a chocolate chunk cookie baked within a brownie tart shell), a sweet and salty caramel brownie, and all of their three-layer cakes. Not content just to bake, the self-proclaimed "gentlemen bakers" have also written four best-selling cookbooks, developed a vintage-inspired bakeware line, and just opened their first shop across the bridge in Tribeca.

—SK

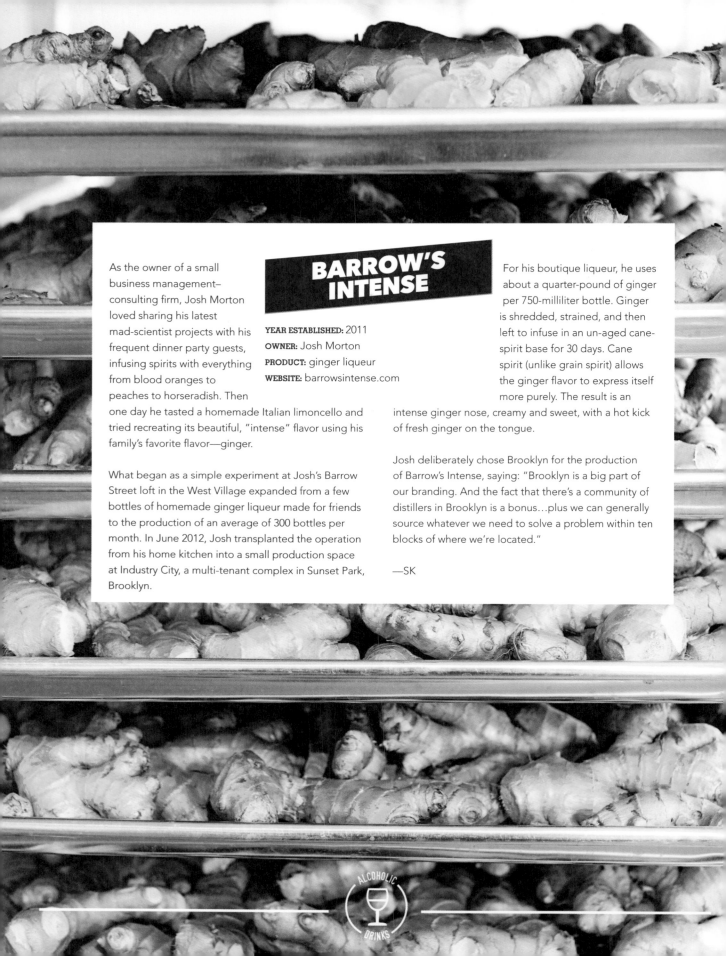

BARROW'S INTENSE

As the owner of a small business management–consulting firm, Josh Morton loved sharing his latest mad-scientist projects with his frequent dinner party guests, infusing spirits with everything from blood oranges to peaches to horseradish. Then one day he tasted a homemade Italian limoncello and tried recreating its beautiful, "intense" flavor using his family's favorite flavor—ginger.

What began as a simple experiment at Josh's Barrow Street loft in the West Village expanded from a few bottles of homemade ginger liqueur made for friends to the production of an average of 300 bottles per month. In June 2012, Josh transplanted the operation from his home kitchen into a small production space at Industry City, a multi-tenant complex in Sunset Park, Brooklyn.

YEAR ESTABLISHED: 2011
OWNER: Josh Morton
PRODUCT: ginger liqueur
WEBSITE: barrowsintense.com

For his boutique liqueur, he uses about a quarter-pound of ginger per 750-milliliter bottle. Ginger is shredded, strained, and then left to infuse in an un-aged cane-spirit base for 30 days. Cane spirit (unlike grain spirit) allows the ginger flavor to express itself more purely. The result is an intense ginger nose, creamy and sweet, with a hot kick of fresh ginger on the tongue.

Josh deliberately chose Brooklyn for the production of Barrow's Intense, saying: "Brooklyn is a big part of our branding. And the fact that there's a community of distillers in Brooklyn is a bonus…plus we can generally source whatever we need to solve a problem within ten blocks of where we're located."

—SK

BELLOCQ TEA ATELIER

YEAR ESTABLISHED: 2010
OWNER: Heidi Johannsen Stewart and Michael Shannon
PRODUCT: tea
WEBSITE: bellocq.com

Hailing from the worlds of decorative arts, architecture, and food styling, longtime friends Heidi Johannsen Stewart and Michael Shannon started Bellocq with the intention of creating high-quality, full-leaf tea blends with natural flavoring, and filling a gap in America's primarily low-grade tea culture.

The intrepid duo, searching for quality ingredients to taste and test themselves, travel to far-flung locations to hand-select full tea leaves and leaf tips from places like Japan, Sri Lanka, China, and India. The results of their expeditions, coupled with Heidi's botanical wizardry at blending such elements as lavender, rose, bergamot, and cedar, are delicious and aromatic, and completely handcrafted. Upon entering Bellocq's tea atelier, located in the busy industrial waterfront community of Greenpoint, one immediately experiences a luxurious world of exotic and earthy scents.

Popular blends include Le Hammeauz (think summer meadow), and White Wolf, a tea dreamt up for winter-centric sipping inspired by expansive western frontiers (imagine hay and saddle, leather and snow). For Heidi, seasonal blends are "poetry, (that) can evoke a feeling and be very transporting."

This precise aesthetic approach can be seen in everything at Bellocq, from the sunflower-yellow connoisseur caddies (tea tins) of their packaging, to the curated feel of the tasting room filled with lavish flower arrangements and decorative arts.

—SK

BIEN CUIT

YEAR ESTABLISHED: 2011
OWNER: Zachary Golper and Kate Wheatcroft
PRODUCT: artisanal bread and pastries
WEBSITE: biencuit.com

Bien cuit means "well done" in French and refers to the dark crust of perfectly baked bread, an appropriate name for the extraordinary Cobble Hill bakery owned by chef Zachary Golper and his wife, Kate Wheatcroft. Employing traditional techniques for small-batch hand mixing and slow fermentation, Zach creates European and American inspired artisanal breads and pastry with patience and precision, evident in each loaf of miche and every double-baked brandy-soaked almond croissant he bakes.

Drawn to Brooklyn in 2011 after reinventing the bread program at Le Bec-Fin in Philadelphia, Zach and Kate settled in Cobble Hill, a tight-knit food community with a large European contingent—the ideal audience for this bakery. Dark crusty loaves of the aforementioned exceptionally delicious miche, potato-spiked pugliese, classic sourdough champagne, toasty rye and sunflower, and others beckon you into their Smith Street shop to gather and connect through the common pleasure of enjoying expertly crafted breads and pastries. And at their commissary in Sunset Park, Bien Cuit bakes for markets and restaurants throughout New York City.

Zach tells a funny story about their first day the bakery opened. Having had no previous experience running a store, Kate hadn't thought to order a safe. So at day's end, the manager wondered what to do with the cash they had earned. Thinking fast on her feet, "[Kate] took a miche down from the bread display, dug out the back, shoved the money in and put the bread back on the shelf." They kept the money like that each night until the safe arrived a week later. They've certainly learned a lot since then.

—MSV

BLUE MARBLE

YEAR ESTABLISHED: 2007
OWNER: Jennifer Dundas and Alexis Miesen
PRODUCT: organic ice cream
WEBSITE: bluemarbleicecream.com

Jennifer Dundas and Alexis Miesen recognized that Brooklynites were hungry for locally sourced, eco-friendly products. So in 2007, they created Blue Marble ice cream, the first certified organic artisanal ice cream made in Brooklyn. They named their company after the Earth itself (think the Big Blue Marble), the spherical shape of a scoop, and their overwhelming interest in the universal impact ice cream can have.

Through their non-profit organization Blue Marble Dreams (www.bluemarbledreams.org), Jennifer and Alexis are "exploring the transformative potential of ice cream not just as a source of fun and joy but also as a means of sustainable economic growth in developing countries with local, but underutilized, dairy resources." In 2010, they opened Inzozi Nziza (Sweet Dreams), the first ice cream shop in Butare, Rwanda. There they employ Rwandan women, support local farmers, and provide the community with a gathering place to nourish their spirits. A similar project is underway in Haiti. Amazing what a scoop of ice cream can do.

Back in Brooklyn, Blue Marble now has two scoop shops and a third in the works at the Industry City Food Hall. Their sense of community and collaboration with other local food artisans, including Good Batch (page 72) and Brooklyn Brewery (page 30), is a testament to their overall mission to use ice cream as a vehicle for good things both near and far.

—MSV

BROOKLYN BREWERY

Brooklyn's history of brewing beer is deep; the large number of German immigrants who arrived in the 19th century brought with them a taste for good beer and the tradition of the Reinheitsgebot, the 1516 German-state beer purity law mandating the use of only hops, malted barley, and water in the making of beer. In the early 1900s, there were no fewer than 48 breweries in Brooklyn; the last family brewery closed in 1976, the final victim of bland, national large-scale beers.

Eight years later: AP correspondent Steve Hindy returns from the Middle East and settles in Park Slope. Hindy, having learned home brewing techniques from diplomats in Islamic countries where alcoholic beverages are forbidden, meets his downstairs neighbor, Tom Potter, a bank officer, who shares his passion for beer. They quit their jobs and pursue their goal of bringing good beer back to New York City. Thus the Brooklyn Brewery (with its

YEAR ESTABLISHED: 1987
OWNER: Eric and Robin Ottaway, Garrett Oliver, and Steve Hindy
PRODUCT: craft beer
WEBSITE: brooklynbrewery.com

distinctive logo by Milton Glaser) was born.

Having grown from a Park Slope basement into an internationally recognized brand now based in Williamsburg, Brooklyn Brewery makes 100,000 barrels of beer annually in the borough (with 160,000 more produced in Utica). Their first, and still best-selling beer, is Brooklyn Lager, based on the all-malt lager beers brewed in Brooklyn in the 19th and early 20th centuries, accounting for half of their total production. The Brooklyn facility also makes five other year-round beers, six seasonal beers, and a range of bottle-conditioned, Belgian-style beers packaged in champagne bottles complete with cork and wire cage. Every quarter, the brewery introduces a new draft beer that demonstrates the versatility and creativity of their famous brewmaster, Garrett Oliver.

—SK

BROOKLYN BRINE

YEAR ESTABLISHED: 2009
OWNER: Shamus Jones
PRODUCT: pickles
WEBSITE: brooklynbrine.com

Growing up in non-gentrified, 80s Brooklyn, Shamus Jones developed an early interest in non-commodified foods, "fueled," as he puts it, by his mother, who avoided large-grocer-stocked factory food products in favor of fresh, directly sourced food. Later, Shamus worked in different vegetarian restaurant kitchens for several years, where pickles often adorned plates. Struck by inspiration, the then 29-year-old Shamus decided to make pickles more than a condiment and began creating his concoctions in various friends' restaurant kitchens.

Today this pickle purveyor occupies a 2,300-square-foot factory in Gowanus, employing six people and churning out 10,000 jars a week, shipping them as far as China, Japan, and South Africa. Last year alone his production grew by 62%.

He is known for eclectic and creative twists on this traditional NYC deli staple, from the award-winning Spicy Maple Bourbon Pickle to red-wine-vinegar-soaked beets with tarragon and fennel seeds. Shamus also pickles cauliflower, sauerkraut, carrots, green beans, and jalapeños, each in its own unique spice blend that's mixed in-house.

Customers are always welcome to come by the Gowanus manufacturing space and soak in the brine permeating the Brooklyn Brine retail shop; home pickling kits are available, and he has now opened up a pickle-centric vegan restaurant, Pickle Shack, just around the corner.

—SK

BROOKLYN CUPCAKE

YEAR ESTABLISHED: 2011
OWNER: Carmen Rodriguez, Gina Madera, and Michelle Caballero
PRODUCT: cupcakes
WEBSITE: brooklyncupcake.com

Brooklyn Cupcake is the small-business success story of two sisters, Carmen Rodriguez and Gina Madera, and their cousin, Michelle Caballero, all born and bred in Williamsburg, Brooklyn. Staying true to what they knew—baking, retail management, and the strength of family and community ties——they transformed an abandoned Greenpoint storefront into a cupcake bakery that has quickly become a favorite of the neighborhood and beyond.

Kudos to Carmen and Gina's mom who knew her girls had the potential to succeed and gave them her life savings so that they could follow their dream of opening their own business. They hit the ground running, creating flavors like tres leches, dulce de leche, flan, guava con queso, conquito rainbow cookie, and tiramisu, each infused with flavors drawn from their Puerto Rican and Italian roots.

Word spread of their one-of-a-kind, urban-inspired cupcakes. Before they knew it, they were competing on the Food Network's *Cupcake Wars*, *The Daily News* had deemed them the best cupcake shop in NYC, and they had earned a glowing Zagat rating. Whole Foods, Gourmet Garage, Barclays Center, and many others have followed, and voilà, business is booming and they've made their mom proud.

—MSV

SWEET FOODS

's where your story begins...
ROOKLYN

BROOKLYN

BROOKLYN HEMISPHERICAL BITTERS

YEAR ESTABLISHED: 2010
OWNER: Mark Buettler
PRODUCT: cocktail bitters
WEBSITE: brooklynbitters.com

The cocktail culture has experienced a revival in the last few years and Brooklyn has been at the forefront of this renaissance. Bitters have made a resurgence too, adding balance and complex, rich, spicy flavors to classic cocktails. While bartending in Williamsburg, mixologist Mark Buettler began experimenting with bitters recipes. The German bitters he was using were expensive to import and he had some new flavor ideas of his own. Bartender friends liked what they tasted and wanted more. So as Mark likes to say, he didn't found Brooklyn Hemispherical Bittters, Brooklyn Hemispherical Bitters found him.

Mark handcrafts his seasonal bitters in the basement of the Greenpoint speakeasy, Featherweight. He macerates botanicals, like barks, roots, and herbs, in high-proof grain alcohol (the higher the proof, the better the flavor absorption), then adds fresh or dried fruits and spices to create four unique flavors: Black Mission Fig, (homemade) Sriracha, Meyer Lemon, and Rhubarb. The attention to detail is what makes these bitters great, from the preparation and seasonality of the ingredients to their dark brown apothecary bottle with a dropper top.

Mark suggests the versatile Sriracha bitters in a Sazarac; Fig with dark rum, American whiskey, or peaty Scotch; Rhubarb to brighten up your next Manhattan; and Meyer Lemon with white-spirit-based drinks such as champagne cocktails and whiskey sours.

—MSV

BROOKLYN ROASTING COMPANY

YEAR ESTABLISHED: 2009
OWNER: Jim Munson and Michael Pollack
PRODUCT: roasted coffee beans and brewed coffee drinks
WEBSITE: brooklynroasting.com

Brooklyn Roasting Company's mission: create coffee blends with the bold, distinctive character found in the neighborhoods and residents of the borough. "We've set ourselves a very high bar," reflects founder Jim Munson over addictively delicious cortados in the roaster's spacious café headquarters: "We aim to be as great as the borough we're named after."

Jim got started early in marketing Brooklyn: one of the first hires at Brooklyn Brewery, he quickly rose to through the ranks, selling an authentic, full-flavored product and bootstrap attitude. He credits his experience (and the guidance of investor Tom Potter, co-founder of the brewery) for providing Brooklyn Roasting's blueprint. After a stint learning the coffee trade, Jim chose Dumbo to start his business because it was zoned for manufacturing and the nation's leading importers and roasters of yore were once based here. The company's HQ is in the old Arbuckle Coffee building.

Brooklyn Roasting roasts some 70,000 pounds per month of a wide variety of superb sustainable coffees, with Mocha Java and Iris Espresso being their most popular blends. The company maintains a strong commitment to individual and small collective growers around the world (many operating at poverty level or lower); 80% of their coffee comes from Fair Trade, Rainforest Alliance, and certified organic crops, which ensures farmers receive fair payment for their harvest.

Ultimately Jim and partner Michael Pollack hope to redefine the commodity-driven coffee industry in America. Their exponential growth and spunky approach to making coffee a way of life may well be close to achieving that: what was a tiny operation at the beginning now boasts more than 100 employees on the wholesale roasting side and five (and counting) branded coffee shops in Brooklyn and Manhattan. That indeed is bold.

—SK

COFFEE, TEA
BEVERAGES

BROOKLYN SODA WORKS

YEAR ESTABLISHED: 2010
OWNER: Caroline Mak and Antonio Ramos
PRODUCT: sodas, sparking juices
WEBSITE: brooklynsodaworks.com

Most people think of soda as flavored sugary syrup with carbonated water. Brooklyn Soda Works has a wholly different and unique approach. They press seasonal, local, fresh fruit juice, steep it with spices and herbs, carbonate it, and keg it. Think beer, but without the alcohol.

Caroline Mak and Antonio Ramos, a former installation artist and research engineer, respectively, are the founders of this one-of-a-kind soda business. Together with their team of dedicated soda makers, they take pride in their ability to figure things out and experiment. Whether it relates to creating exciting taste profiles or improving production equipment to keep up with demand, the crew at Brooklyn Soda Works has all the bases covered.

Though ginger plays a staring role in their kitchen—Apple & Ginger is the most popular flavor and the first to be bottled and available for retail—adventurous ingredients and flavor combinations like Watermelon & Tarragon; Red Currant & Shiso; and Grapefruit, Jalapeno & Honey are what make Brooklyn Soda Works special. Find these and many others on tap at local restaurants and bars.

—MSV

BROOKLYN WOK SHOP

YEAR ESTABLISHED: 2011
OWNER: Edric and Melissa Har
PRODUCT: chili oil
WEBSITE: brooklynwokshop.com

Edric Har serves his signature Brooklyn Wok Shop Chili Oil at the Williamsburg restaurant he owns with his wife, Melissa. The spicy, garlicky, savory oil adds fantastic flavor to Edric's upscale takes on traditional Cantonese dishes.

When the Hars moved to Brooklyn from Manhattan in 2010, they missed their local take-out spots and were unimpressed with the Chinese food options in the neighborhood. So Edric took matters into his own hands. Combining memories of his Chinatown upbringing with his well-honed culinary skills as a chef in some of New York's most respected kitchens (Le Bernardin, Veritas, and Cru), Edric created Chinese food 2.0 at Brooklyn Wok Shop. He uses only hormone and antibiotic free poultry and pork, makes stock and egg noodles from scratch, and never uses MSG!

Brooklyn Wok Shop Chili Oil is wonderful as a dipping sauce for grilled meats or as a marinade for meat and poultry. I like it added to clam chowder, drizzled on omelets and avocado sandwiches, and with just about anything else I can think of.

—MSV

BUENA VISTA TORTILLAS

YEAR ESTABLISHED: 1994
OWNER: Noe Baltazar
PRODUCT: tortillas and tostadas

I was first introduced to the tostadas from Buena Vista Tortillas one morning when the photographer of this book, Heather Weston, kindly made me breakfast. She scrambled up some eggs, added a dash of tomatillo salsa, and a tostada on the side. From the very first bite, I was hooked. The toasted sweet corn taste of the perfectly crisp golden disk was like no other I'd had before and I needed more. So what better than to go right to the source?

Buena Vista Tortillas is located in between the neighborhoods of East Williamsburg and Bushwick, in what some refer to as the "tortilla triangle" for the cluster of tortilla factories located there. Beginning in the 1990s, great numbers of Mexican immigrants settled in these neighborhoods and began manufacturing Mexican products that were hard to find locally. Made from masa and water, the dough is fed into large tortilla machines that flatten, cut, and cook the tortillas on long conveyor belts, churning out more than 1 million tortillas and tostadas every day. I couldn't resist grabbing one directly from the belt and popping it in my mouth before it reached the end to be bagged.

Buena Vista is strictly a factory, their tortillas are sold in bodegas throughout the city. Another tortilla maker, Tortilla Mexicana Los Hermanos, is just a few blocks away and has a tiny cantina carved out of a corner of their factory floor. Authentic Mexican favorites like carnitas and chorizo tacos are wrapped in their fragrant, hot, chewy corn tortillas. It doesn't get any fresher than this.

—MSV

45

BUTTER & SCOTCH

YEAR ESTABLISHED: 2012
OWNER: Keavy Blueher and Allison Kave
PRODUCT: desserts

Cupcake specialist Keavy Blueher (of Kumquat Cupcakery) and pie professional Allison Kave (of First Prize Pies) met through a mutual love of baking and booze. In 2012, they teamed up to start Butter & Scotch and in January 2015, they opened a lounge of the same name. They serve fabulous craft cocktails and classic American desserts reinvented with a boozy riff. Their Bourbon Ginger Pecan Pie is a standout, as are the acclaimed S'mores Pie and Maple Bacon Cupcakes. And don't miss their endlessly snackable Cocktail Caramel Corn in flavors like the addictive Dark & Stormy, crave-worthy Green Chili Margarita, and comforting Hot Toddy.

They have also created a line of playfully boozy pies—the Bourbon Ginger Pecan Pie is a standout—as is the famed S'mores Pie. And of course they make cupcakes, too! No trip to Butter & Scotch is complete without a taste of at least one—choose from Maple Bacon, Lemon Lavender, Coffee Caramel Bourbon, Chocolate Orange, and Peanut Butter Banana Honey.

—SK

CACAO PRIETO

YEAR ESTABLISHED: 2010
OWNER: Daniel Prieto Preston
PRODUCT: organic beans-to-bar chocolate;
cacao-based liqueur and rum
WEBSITE: cacaoprieto.com

Daniel Prieto Preston, a prolific inventor (more than 100 patents and pending patents) and former aerospace engineer, founded Cacao Prieto after selling his parachute company for a tidy sum (he invented a military-grade system after a close call with a failed parachute). His unlikely source of inspiration? His family's hundred-year-old organic cacao plantation in the Dominican Republic. Cacao Prieto is one of the few chocolate companies worldwide that is completely vertically integrated from the farm to the finished product.

Daniel repurposed three impressive, conjoining brick buildings in sparse, industrial Red Hook, into a mature, modern-day facility: a chocolate factory of custom-made machines roasting, mixing, and extruding delicious chocolate treats. The site even contains Botanica, an exquisitely appointed tasting room, and a courtyard full of eccentric chickens. And if this weren't enough, he launched a bean-to-bottle spirit distillery of fine cacao-based liqueur and quite delicious rum.

Daniel's other projects are Brooklyn Cacao, which designs and manufactures chocolate machines, and Widow Jane (page 190), a distiller of heirloom bourbon whiskey. He has also developed a unique controlled fermentation process for the cacao, and invented a vortex winnower to separate cacao bibs from the shell. Cacao Prieto is a magical place of ideas, traditions, dreams, and technology devoted to the delicious art and science of the wonderful world of chocolate.

—SK

SWEET FOODS · ALCOHOLIC DRINKS

CACAO PRIETO

CACAO PRIETO

CACAO PRIETO

CAFÉ GRUMPY

YEAR ESTABLISHED: 2005
OWNER: Chris Timbrell and Caroline Bell
PRODUCT: coffee

In 2005, husband and wife Chris Timbrell and Caroline Bell dreamed of starting a neighborhood-focused corner coffee spot. With a name and logo inspired by a cantankerous-looking coffee bean, they opened Café Grumpy in Greenpoint. In the years since, Café Grumpy has become one of the city's best-regarded coffee brands and developed an avid following among NYC's coffee aficionados due to its constantly rotating menu of single-origin brews. Today there are half a dozen Grumpy cafes strewn across Brooklyn and Manhattan, and the couple founded their own roastery and bakery in 2009.

Their roastery is located in Greenpoint, where their original, lovingly restored, vintage 15-kilo Probat L12 roaster has been joined by a new 45-kilo G45 Probat to accommodate the increased demands of their mini-chain and growing list of wholesale customers.

Despite their brush with pop-culture fame due to the shop's appearance on HBO's *Girls*, Caroline and Chris stay true to their original goal to simply serve and make good coffee.

—SK

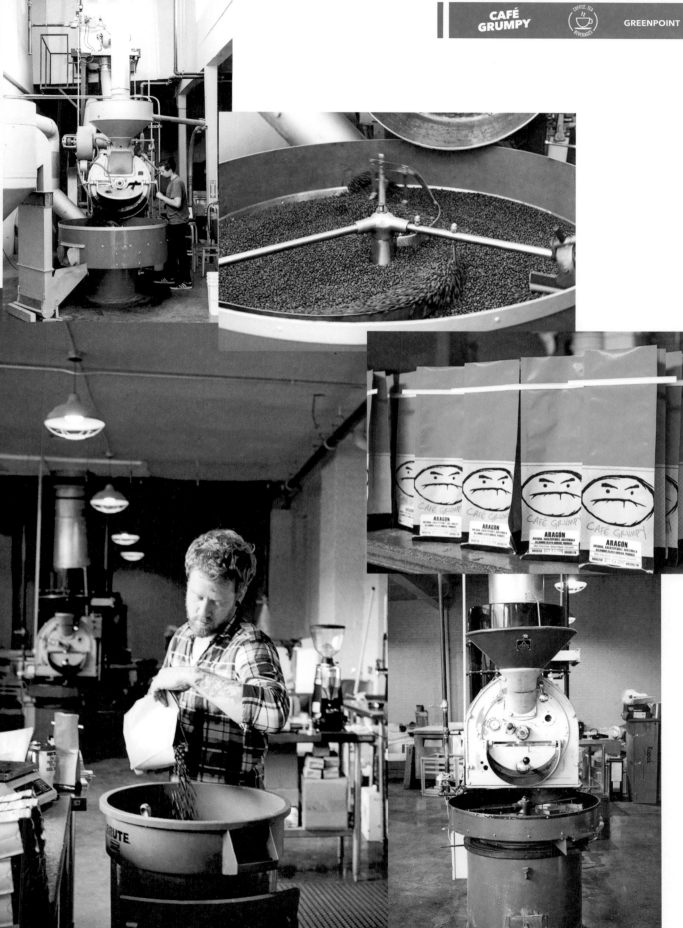

Everything Deborah Williamson touches is graced with simple elegance and sophisticated design. In 2008, she opened James—the Prospect Heights farm-to-table restaurant she owns with her chef husband, Bryan Calvert—a gray-washed, lilac-infused, neighborhood favorite. Four years later, Deborah and Bryan created Cecil & Merl, a line of hand-crafted artisanal goods, spreading their passion for local, sustainable foods beyond the doors of James.

Cecil & Merl first launched with their signature lemon ricotta cheesecakes: rustic loaves made with light and creamy ricotta, local eggs, organic milk, and a graham cracker crust on three sides. The line has expanded to include tart mango, sweet and salty dulce de leche,

CECIL & MERL

YEAR ESTABLISHED: 2012
OWNER: Deborah Williamson and Bryan Calvert, and Justin Lane Briggs, who makes the bitters
PRODUCT: bitters, cheesecake
WEBSITE: cecilandmerl.com

seasonal spicy pumpkin, and a gluten-free version. If cheesecake is your jam, you've got to try these.

A collaboration with James cocktail guru Justin Lang Briggs added handcrafted cherry and apricot bitters to the mix. Justin believes bitters should be part of everyone's cocktail repertoire. But his interest and understanding of the agricultural roots (no pun intended) of the individual ingredients allows him to derive intense flavors from macerating roots, spices, herbs, bing cherries, and organic apricots in high-proof alcohol.

Cecil & Merl also makes a signature black market tote bag, designed to carry all your goodies in style.

—MSV

COLSON PATISSERIE

YEAR ESTABLISHED: 2006
OWNER: Yonatan Israel
PRODUCT: French and Belgian pastries
WEBSITE: colsonpatisserie.com

Park Slope is home to Colson Patisserie, a European bakeshop serving handmade French and Belgian breakfast pastries and a rotating selection of meticulously prepared tarts and desserts. Owner Yonatan Israel, a Parisian-born filmmaker, opened the patisserie in 2006 to celebrate the recipes and traditions of Hubert Colson, a renowned Belgian pastry chef and family friend. Expertly crafted waffles, croissants, and financiers fill the case at Colson's quaint corner shop, which features local art adorning the walls and a Parisian-style menu painted on an enormous mirrored wall.

But Park Slope couldn't claim Colson as its little secret forever. Word spread of perfectly light and buttery croissants, and soon wholesale requests came, literally, knocking on their door. Yonatan obliged and, in order to keep up with the demand, opened Colson's second location in the Food Hall at Industry City in Sunset Park. Here they have a large commissary kitchen and a small café, catering to their Industry City neighbors. They send out thousands of boxes of freshly baked goodness every morning to shops, markets, and restaurants all across New York City.

And every few months, Hubert Colson comes to Brooklyn to check in on Yonatan and his staff. Together they fine-tune their techniques, create new recipes, and perfect the artistry that Yonatan learned from his Belgian mentor more than a decade ago.

—MSV

CRACKED CANDY

YEAR ESTABLISHED: 2013
OWNER: Flora Pringle
PRODUCT: sugar-free candy
WEBSITE: crackedcandy.com

Imagine an Australian high-school science teacher transplanted to Brooklyn with a baby and a heavy craving for sugar, give her lots of free time to investigate and experiment, a burning desire to make the perfect sugar-free candy, and several months in her Brooklyn Heights kitchen until she cracks the code— and you have it: an unconventional, healthy, handmade, sugar-free treat called Cracked Candy, concocted by Flora Pringle.

The secret to Cracked Candy is xylitol, a naturally occurring sweetener that contains a third fewer calories than sugar. Cracked Candy's xylitol is non-GMO and sourced from birch trees; diabetic-safe and enamel-friendly (bacteria in our mouths cannot metabolize the compound, and they die off), the substance is incredibly light, sweet, and yummy. Cracked Candy is made with therapeutic-grade essential oils and xylitol, which are spread onto sheets, cooled, and then smashed by hand into shards of varying sizes. You can choose what size to pop into your mouth depending on your mood.

Cracked Candy comes in four mouth-tingling flavors: Lemon Ice, Peppermint Ice, Cinnamon, and Mellow Orange, each packed in a colorful tin designed by Flora's art director husband Nick.

—SK

CRACKED CANDY

CRACKED CANDY

CRACKED CANDY

CRACKED CANDY

DAMASCUS BAKERY

YEAR ESTABLISHED: 1930
OWNER: Edward and David Mafoud
PRODUCT: pita, flat breads
WEBSITE: damascusbakery.com

Damascus is a third-generation family-owned bakery founded in 1930 by Hassan Halaby, a young Syrian immigrant who arrived in America with the intention of becoming a surgeon. Money being tight, he ended up opening a tailoring shop (having learned the trade from his Syrian family). Hassan found the most enjoyment, however, in his off-hours, baking Syrian breads. Fast forward, and the bakery Damascus was born.

Hassan's business began booming after the Depression ended. His reputation for baking delectable bread was spread through word of mouth by the many artists, writers, and artisans who frequented or moved into his Brooklyn Heights neighborhood.

In 1966, his son Henry Halaby and son-in-law Anthony Mafoud entered into partnership. Eventually the brothers-in-law divided their duties, and Henry continued to run the original retail store on Atlantic Avenue, while Tony devoted himself to manufacturing bread in his factory on Gold Street in Vinegar Hill. Mafoud went on to build the first automated pita bread factory in the United States. Today his sons, Edward and David, are proud to be the third generation of family members operating Damascus Bakery, offering pita, lavash wraps, and roll-ups, as well as other artisanal flatbreads such as paninis, pizza crusts, and breadsticks.

—SK

DOC'S ALL NATURAL SPIRITS

YEAR ESTABLISHED: 2012

OWNER: Kevin Herson and Stacey Luckow

PRODUCT: absinthe

WEBSITE: docsspirits.com

Absinthe, referred to in literature as "the green fairy" may be the most misunderstood spirit in history. Although it was successfully used as a malaria suppressant for French soldiers in the 1840s, the belief that drinking absinthe induced hallucinogenic, mind-altering episodes dominated the culture of the time. The chemical thujone, a derivative of wormwood, one of absinthe's key ingredients, was blamed. And the revolutionary impressionist paintings of famous absinthe drinkers like Degas, Van Gough, Toulouse-Lautrec, and others only bolstered prohibitionist's beliefs. As a result, absinthe was banned in many countries, including the United States, from 1912 until 2007. But eventually science prevailed. Only traces of thujone actually exist in wormwood and it was more likely that other additives and excessive drinking caused any psychoactive effects.

More recently, a dapper pair of California transplants, Kevin Herson and Stacey Luckow, found absinthe intriguing and decided to try their hand at small-batch distilling. They established Doc's All Natural Spirits, the first absinthe distillery in New York, in a quiet corner of the Pfizer building.

Production of one batch of absinthe is a long and detailed process, done entirely by Kevin, that involves fermentation of organic New York State grains, two distillations, and the processing of ten dried botanicals and fresh mint leaves for color and flavor. Bottled, hand labeled, and wax sealed, this glorious green, minty spirit will make anyone an absinthe devotee. For more details on the fascinating process and how Kevin and Stacey became distillers, take a seat at Doc's bar, set up on weekends in the doorway of the distillery, sip some absinthe, and chat with them while they work.

—MSV

ALCOHOLIC DRINKS

DOUGH

YEAR ESTABLISHED: 2010
OWNER: Fany Gerson
PRODUCT: doughnuts
WEBSITE: doughbrooklyn.com

Fany Gerson is a busy person. Running two successful Brooklyn-based food businesses, La Newyorkina (page 108) and Dough, leaves little time for much else, including sleep! But this Mexico City native loves what she does and that's evident the minute you bite into the perfectly fried, enormous-yet-surprisingly-light, glazed, yeast doughnuts at Dough. Think of them as a celebration of something special that shouldn't end too soon.

Adorable in her braids and bandana, Fany spent months testing and tweaking to achieve her ideal doughnut before opening her first shop on a once deserted corner of Lafayette and Franklin Avenues. The store's rough-hewn atmosphere, with windows into the kitchen and sweet smells wafting through the air, welcomes you in to choose from innovative flavors like chocolate salted caramel, passion fruit, hibiscus, and dulce de leche with toasted almonds, or classics like plain glazed and cinnamon sugar.

Her modern takes on this time-honored favorite are handcrafted throughout the day at her Bed-Stuy and Chelsea (NYC) shops. So it's guaranteed yours will always be warm, fresh, and bursting with artisanal passion and goodness. Dough doughnuts are also sold at the Brooklyn Flea, Smorgasburg, and various markets throughout the city.

—MSV

EARLY BIRD FOODS & CO.

YEAR ESTABLISHED: 2009
OWNER: Nekisia Davis
PRODUCT: granola
WEBSITE: earlybirdfoods.com

Nekisia Davis was at the forefront of the New Brooklyn food movement, and among the select few to have a food stand at the first Brooklyn Flea (page 196). She debuted her Early Bird granola in three addictive flavors, while working front-of-the-house at Franny's in Prospect Heights. Today, her granola is sold nationwide, as well as in Europe and Japan, and has expanded to six flavors and two breakfast bars. But some wonderful things remain the same. Every batch is still made with her signature combination of fruity extra-virgin olive oil, salt, and a whole lot of love.

The name Early Bird evokes life on a farm and the fruit crate graphics exude a rustic urban charm, hinting at the handmade wholesome goodness in each bag. Sweet, salty, crunchy, and nutty, Early Bird granolas are full of rich, savory flavor with just the right amount of spice. Nekisia starts with raw nuts, raw seeds, and local and organic ingredients whenever possible. Combined with maple syrup, brown sugar, and olive oil, each bite of her granola is well balanced and perfectly crispy.

Based in Red Hook, Early Bird shares space with three other Brooklyn makers, Salvatore Ricotta (page 162), The White Moustache (page 176) and Tin Mustard (page 193). This small-batch food factory has true Brooklyn-maker spirit written all over it, with artisans supporting each other's entrepreneurial efforts every step of the way. Nekisia couldn't be happier. "I wasn't born here, but I got here as fast as I could," she says of her beloved Brooklyn. And of Red Hook, "It is the understatement of the century to say that I love it. The water, the sunsets, the people, the businesses, the farm, the bars. There's also something about it that's special because it's not very easy to get to. Everyone here *wants* to be here." Lucky for her, she lives above the kitchen and never has to leave.

—MSV

FINE & RAW

YEAR ESTABLISHED: 2008
OWNER: Daniel Sklaar
PRODUCT: chocolate
WEBSITE: fineandraw.com

Daniel Sklaar describes his chocolate company best: "FINE & RAW is a carefully chaotic celebration of life!" Originally a financial analyst and a self-described rebel and fussitarian, Daniel left Wall Street to pursue the pleasurable world of chocolate. "Possessed as a baby by the chocolate gods," Daniel studied to become a raw chef and applies the techniques he learned to make raw bean-to-bar chocolate bars, truffles, and "chunkys."

Daniel and his crew are creative, innovative, and head-over-heels for chocolate. They craft artisan confections, using organic ingredients, and cook them at low temperatures to keep the chocolate's raw vitality and natural flavor intact. All this happens in a former garage in Bushwick. Daniel worked for several years to transform the space into a working chocolate factory and café. The brick walls, loft offices, glass-enclosed tempering room, and kitchen space have a vibe and flow that suits his style perfectly.
And the chocolate—void of dairy, refined sugars, or anything artificial—is a gratifying eating experience for your senses, and physiologically nourishing, too. One last note, the packaging is fun—different pin-up tattoo-style illustrations adorn each bar—and reminds us that hipster chic is still alive and well.

—MSV

FOX'S U-BET

There is nothing that says old-school Brooklyn more than a classic egg cream, a nostalgic concoction that contains neither eggs nor cream. Every neighborhood candy store and luncheonette once served this soda fountain treat made with milk, seltzer, and chocolate syrup—and not just any chocolate syrup. No respectable egg cream was made with anything other than a healthy dose of Brooklyn's own Fox's U-Bet Chocolate Syrup.

Herman Fox began making Fox's Chocolate Syrup in the basement of his Brownsville brownstone in 1900. Twenty years later, after traveling to Texas in the hope of getting rich drilling oil, Herman returned home broke, but with the oilman's expression "you bet.'" He renamed his product and never looked back. Today, H. Fox & Company is run by third and fourth generation members of the Fox family, David Fox (grandson of Herman) and Kelly Fox (son of David). And

YEAR ESTABLISHED: 1900
OWNER: David Fox
PRODUCT: chocolate syrup
WEBSITE: foxsyrups.com

Brownsville is still home to this old-line manufacturer of tasty memories.

If you are an egg cream purist, look for kosher bottles of U-Bet available each spring for Passover. That's the only time of year they use the original cane sugar and not corn syrup. And once you've got this iconic syrup in hand, follow this recipe and step back into an era gone by.

Original Brooklyn Egg Cream:
Take a tall, chilled, straight-sided, 8-ounce glass: Spoon in an inch of U-Bet chocolate syrup, add an inch of whole milk, then tilt the glass and spray seltzer (from a pressurized cylinder only) onto the bowl of the spoon to make a big, foamy chocolate head. Stir, drink, enjoy!

—MSV

H. FOX & CO., INC.

GILLIES COFFEE COMPANY

YEAR ESTABLISHED: 1840
OWNER: Donald Schoenholt and Hy Chabbott
PRODUCT: coffee
WEBSITE: gilliescoffeee.com

Gillies Coffee Company, one of New York's oldest businesses, was founded in 1840, hence the company's slogan, "America's oldest coffee merchant." Gillies has been championing specialty coffee since the days of clipper ships. In 1838, Wright Gillies, a 17-year-old son of Scottish immigrants, was sent down the river from his parents' farm in Newburgh, New York, to seek his fortune in the city. Two years later he opened up his own tea and coffee business on Washington Street in lower Manhattan, where he installed a horse-powered coffee roaster. His business prospered, eventually supplying retailers as far away as New Orleans. Gillies' innovations included roasting with natural gas, and he was awarded a U.S. patent for the dark "double roasting" process.

During World War II, the Schoenholt family, which was active in the New York coffee trade, acquired Gillies. Donald Schoenholt, the current head of the house, learned the trade at his father's knee, cupping at age 11, and roasting at 14. Almost 25 years ago, Gillies moved its operations to Brooklyn from Manhattan at the suggestion of the Koch administration, which presciently thought that the area around Sunset Industrial Park would be a welcoming neighborhood for new businesses.

Today Gillies is widely known, working with restaurateurs and roasting retailers, cafés and specialty food stores, and creating custom blends for such luminaries as Jacques Torres, River Café, and the Mud Coffee Trucks.

—SK

BEAN ELEVATOR

SMOKELESS ROASTER

GILLIES COFFEE CO.
150   AMERICA'S OLDEST COFFEE MERCHANT   150

NO PARKING

COLOMBIA

THE GOOD BATCH

YEAR ESTABLISHED: 2010
OWNER: Anna Gordon and Steven Hartong
PRODUCT: baked goods, ice cream sandwiches
WEBSITE: thegoodbatch.com

Anna Gordon, owner of the Good Batch and pastry chef extraordinaire, credits her business partner and husband Steven Hartong's Dutch heritage with the impetus to start their company. Steven and his relatives loved stroopwafels, a classic Dutch treat of gooey caramel sandwiched between two wafer cookies, but they couldn't find good ones in the United States. Anna set out to satisfy their craving and, after much tinkering, came up with a winner.

Fresh out of pastry school, Anna came to the Brooklyn Flea, stroopwafels in hand, and people were instantly hooked. The Good Batch was born and quickly expanded their line to include other stroopwafels—cocoa caramel, bonfire, and honey bear; cookies, like oat chocolate chunk, righteous raisin, and ginger molasses; and, to our delight, their now-famous ice cream sandwiches (made with Brooklyn-based Blue Marble ice cream, see page 15). The lines for these babies are still a mile long at the Flea and Smorgasburg, but well worth the wait.

Or you can stop by The Good Batch's year-old Clinton Hill bakery, a welcoming, sweet-smelling spot tiled in Tiffany-blue and white, to enjoy all their classics and more, while Anna and her staff churn out thousands and thousands of delicious cookies (and pies and cakes and more) a day. Anna and Steven live around the corner to be close to the store and love the rich culture and diversity of their neighborhood, a rapidly evolving community of which they have become a sweet part.

—MSV

GORILLA COFFEE

YEAR ESTABLISHED: 2002
OWNER: Carol McLaughlin
PRODUCT: coffee
WEBSITE: gorillacoffee.com

September 11, 2001 was a turning point for many soon-to-be Brooklyn makers. They lost so much and yet simultaneously found, in the face of terror and tragedy, a desire to pursue entrepreneurial projects that "took them back to the idea of homey, I'm going to make you something and I'm glad you like it," Carol McLaughlin says. "And I want to make you something again tomorrow."

This artisan spirit, and Carol's infectious enthusiasm for coffee and those who drink it, remain the driving force behind Gorilla Coffee, the micro-roastery she and a founding partner established in 2002. Gorilla Coffee, like the name, is robust in flavor and boldly represented by its now-iconic red and black graphics. Ethically sourced beans from cooperative family farms in Central and South America, East Africa, and Indonesia are roasted with precision in Gorilla's Sunset Park warehouse and served at their two Park Slope coffee shops.

The newer of the two stores, on Bergen Street, is designed specifically around the desire to offer the customer accessibility and the chance to gain a bit of java knowledge about what they're drinking. Employing several pieces of high-tech machinery—an Italian-made espresso machine by La Marzocco called the Strada EP, and a newfangled American espresso and steam system called Modbar, which hides the bulkier components of traditional espresso machines under the counter—the barista is able to pull single-origin drinks up close and personal to the customers. While the Gorilla approach is refined and sophisticated, Carol and her staff of skilled and passionate roasters and baristas remain true to their original mission, to bring great and accessible coffee to the people of Brooklyn.

—MSV

GOTHAM GREENS

YEAR ESTABLISHED: 2009
OWNER: Viraj Puri and Eric Haley
PRODUCT: herbs, tomatoes, leafy greens
WEBSITE: gothamgreens.com

Stop for a moment and consider all the underused rooftop real estate in our great urban jungle. Now imagine those rooftops covered with glass houses. And inside those glass houses, a sea of fragrant sweet basil as far as the eye can see, rows of peppery arugula, baby's-bottom soft butterhead lettuce, and tomatoes ripe for the picking—growing all year round—harvested before breakfast and delivered to your local market by lunch.

Look no further. Viraj Puri and Eric Haley, CEO and CFO of Gotham Greens, are worldwide pioneers in the field of urban agriculture producing premium-quality, greenhouse-grown pesticide and contaminant-free vegetables and herbs sold to stores, restaurants, and other local retailers within a 20-mile radius of their rooftop farms in Brooklyn (Gowanus and Greenpoint) and Queens (Jamaica). Gotham Greens' pesticide-free produce is grown using ecologically sustainable methods (insects are used as pest control, and all the water they use for irrigation is collected and recycled) in clean-tech, climate-controlled, automated greenhouses. And their yield is a whopping 20 times that of a traditional farm, using a tenth of the water.

The technology may be sophisticated, but it's actually quite simple to understand once you taste Gotham Greens' Basil, Blooming Brooklyn Iceberg and the other hyper-local produce they grow. This is the future of urban farming and it is smart, green, and oh, so delicious.

—MSV

GRADY'S COLD BREW

YEAR ESTABLISHED: 2011
OWNER: Grady Laird, Dave Sands, and Kyle Buckley
PRODUCT: cold-brew coffee
WEBSITE: gradyscoldbrew.com

I know the secret to the perfect iced coffee. It comes in a bottle and, of course, is made in Brooklyn. My love for Grady's Cold Brew is deep and strong. From the first smooth, rich New Orleans' style sweet chicory taste to the lasting caffeine-induced rush, I can't sing Grady's praises enough.

This cold-brew coffee concentrate is made by Grady Laird, Dave Sands, and Kyle Buckley in their "brew compound" in Greenpoint. Striving to offer high-quality, coffee-shop coffee at convenience-store prices, they combine coffee beans from New York roaster Porto Rico, chicory, and spices with room-temperature water, soak it overnight, then hand press, filter, and bottle. Poured over ice and mixed in a one to one ratio with water or milk, Grady's is the ultimate iced coffee in your own fridge.

But that's not all. Want to be a part of the cold-brew experience without all the hands-on? The guys behind Grady's have created Bean Bags, big tea bags filled with their iced coffee recipe. Just soak overnight and wake up to the same bottled cold brew you know and love.

—MSV

GRANOLA LAB

YEAR ESTABLISHED: 2010
OWNER: Alex Crosier
PRODUCT: granola
WEBSITE: granolalab.com

Former neuroscience major and college librarian Alex Crosier had dreams of opening a coffee bar. And the granola she made for friends and family seemed the perfect thing to serve in said future coffee bar. So she set out testing her recipe and sharing it with patrons at a local bar who returned with positive feedback and encouragement to forge ahead. In her spare time, Alex established Granola Lab, named to honor the kitchen as a place of experimentation where, through trial and error, yummy things are perfected.

Alex created five unique and not too sweet, boldly flavored varieties—Activation Energy (my fave), Cranberry-Cashew Compound, Elemental Formula, Get Gingersnapping, and Tamarind Fusion. All are jam-packed with healthy nuts, seeds, dried fruit, and just the right amount of oats. Alex bakes in small batches to keep the mixtures crisp and tasting of home cooking. She also makes Brewers Bars with fruit, seeds, and spent grains of leftover barley malt from the beer brewing process at Brooklyn-based Kelso Brewing. A great Brooklyn makers collaboration.

—MSV

SWEET

GREENHOOK GINSMITHS

YEAR ESTABLISHED: 2012
OWNER: Steve DeAngelo
PRODUCT: gin
WEBSITE: greenhookgin.com

On an industrial block in Greenpoint you'll find the boutique distillery Greenhook Ginsmiths, where owner Steven DeAngelo and distiller Joe O'Sullivan make small-batch artisanal gin. Employing a special process called vacuum distillation, air pressure is removed from their custom 300-liter copper-pot still during distillation, allowing them to distill at low temperatures. This prevents the demise of the delicate flowers, herbs, and spices being infused into the alcohol and results in a highly aromatic and vibrant gin.

Like many of the other artisan makers in this book, Steve is self-taught. He left a career on Wall Street after the 2008 crash and armed with experience drinking gin, a head for numbers, and a business plan, set out to learn the art of distilling. He teamed up with Joe who had extensive distilling experience, and his brother Philip, and four years later, released his first bottles to the public.

Greenhook Ginsmiths currently has three gins to choose from, American Dry Gin, a full flavored spicy yet smooth gin made with the perfect blend of Tuscan juniper, organic elderflower, organic chamomile, and Ceylon cinnamon; Beach Plum Gin Liqueur, a sweet full bodied take on British sloe gin crafted by soaking Long Island wild beach plums in American Dry Gin for seven months; and Old Tom Gin, a style of gin commonly drank in 18th-century England. Steven ages his for one year in bourbon and sherry casks.

—MSV

GREENPOINT TRADING CO.

YEAR ESTABLISHED: 2010
OWNER: Kimmee Arndt and Evan Hoffman
PRODUCT: spices and seasonings
WEBSITE: greenpointtrading.co

Step off a quiet Greenpoint street into the warehouse of Greenpoint Trading Company/Brooklyn Spice Company and you will find your olfactory senses awakened, transporting you to an exotic spice market somewhere far from Brooklyn. Cardamom, cumin, and garlic permeate the air in this space, where husband and wife team Kimmee Arndt and Evan Hoffman create custom spice blends for retail and wholesale customers.

Jump back a few years to 2011, when Evan decided to parlay seven years of spice experience gained working for others into a classic mom-and-pop start-up with his then-girlfriend, Kimmee. And like many other local food makers, they began at home, lining their apartment hallways with bulk spices and inviting friends and family over for packaging parties. They debuted their signature spice blends at local farmers' markets and people fell in love.

Back to the present, and they've moved into a great old warehouse, now lined with pallets of bulk spices. They buy direct from importers and hand-mix their cleverly named blends like Dracula's Nightmare (a salt-free garlic seasoning), All Aboard for Seafood, Chick'n Little for poultry, and the oh-so-popular Roasted Garlic Pepper Seasoning & Coffee Rub, a double dose of garlic mixed with coffee grounds from local roaster Toby's Estate.

—MSV

INDUSTRY CITY DISTILLERY

YEAR ESTABLISHED: 2011
OWNER: David Kyrejko and Zachary Bruner
PRODUCT: vodka
WEBSITE: drinkicd.com

Visit Industry City Distilling's 12,000-square-foot warehouse loft in the old Bush Terminal (now renamed Industry City) in Sunset Park and you understand right away that this is a mind-blowing operation. David and Zachary (whose engineering backgrounds are evident) oversee a vast space that is part biotech lab/part machine shop. Witness their specific reason for distilling vodka: "We make booze to pay for projects in art and science." Industry City Distillery is just one of the projects they've undertaken through their main venture, The City Foundry, a research and development collective that focuses on energy efficiency and the creation of sustainable urban technologies.

Since 2011, The City Foundry has reinvented the distilling process and developed five new technologies, from ultraviolet sterilization and immobilized cell bioreactors to a custom-built system that suspends the yeast that drives fermentation. David and Zachary even make their own yeast with algae, and they ferment beet sugar before distilling the vodka. Their vodka is made entirely with equipment designed and fabricated right at their warehouse space, making them the only distillery to use stills designed and built in New York City in more than 100 years.

Though they claim their vodka is just a byproduct, Industry City Distilling makes one of the smoothest tasting vodkas around. David and Zachary achieve the dense palate of flavors of their sugar beet vodka, Industry Standard, by tasting all 40 cuts and then mixing the most usable ones into their formula, unlike traditional distillers, who toss the alcohol–rich "head" and the heavy-flavored "tails" of their still-runs. They also developed a totally neutral 191.2 proof spirit called Technical Reserve, the first ever designed for creating bitters, tinctures, and infusions where totally neutral, high proof spirits are essential.

—SK

INDUSTRY CITY
DISTILLERY

INDUSTRY CITY
DISTILLERY

ALCOHOLIC
DRINKS

SUNSET
PARK

J.W. OVERBEY & CO.

YEAR ESTABLISHED: 2013
OWNER: Joseph Overbey
PRODUCT: bourbon
WEBSITE: jwoverbey.com

In a 580-square foot corner on the eighth floor of the Pfizer Building, Tennessee native Joseph Overbey is making bourbon. Mashed, fermented, barrel-aged, and bottled in his urban micro distillery, this bourbon uses local corn and malted barley, both organic grains from New York State. Aged four to six months in five-gallon barrels, Joseph's bourbon benefits from lots of surface area of wood to spirit, and maximizes the extraction of the characteristics of the barrel, imparting delicious flavor into his slightly sweet, nutty whiskey.

Joseph grew up around people making stuff. His father built houses, his mother is a jewelry designer, and his grandmother, with whom he spent a lot of his time, lived on "a very productive piece of land" with apple orchards, cherry trees, vegetable gardens, and corn fields. So the do-it-yourself spirit is in his blood. After moving from a kitchenless apartment in Manhattan to new Brooklyn digs, Joseph's love for cooking, fermenting, and distilling had proper room to blossom again and, luckily for us, inspired him to try his hand at producing a commercially viable craft spirit.

Joseph is patient and focused, eager to experiment and happy to allow the layered and meticulous process work its magic. We're excited to see what's next for J.W. Overbey. Meanwhile, drinking Manhattans made with his bourbon will keep us sated for now.

—MSV

ALCOHOLIC DRINKS

JACK FROM BROOKLYN

YEAR ESTABLISHED: 2012
OWNER: Jack Summers
PRODUCT: hibiscus liqueur
WEBSITE: jackfrombrooklyn.com

Caribbean Islanders have been making sorrel for centuries. Jack Summer's Sorel liqueur, steeped and blended in Red Hook, salutes that time-honored tradition and combines the warm aromatic flavors of hibiscus, nutmeg, ginger, clove, cinnamon, and cassis with pure organic grain alcohol to create a complex, layered, sweet-but-not-cloying delight.

A cancer scare in 2010 sparked Jack's desire, simply put, to day drink, and ultimately, after 20 years of making sorrel for friends and family, he was inspired to launch his own brand in early 2012. Then, like most of Red Hook, Jack's distillery drowned under six feet of water from Hurricane Sandy, but he overcame that too.

"There's nothing noble about what I do," Jack says. We wholeheartedly disagree. The small-batch, artisanal spiced liqueur is a deep-pink drinking revelation infused with the energy, passion, and vibrant spirit of its maker. Enjoy it cold, hot, mixed, or neat.

—MSV

ALCOHOLIC DRINKS

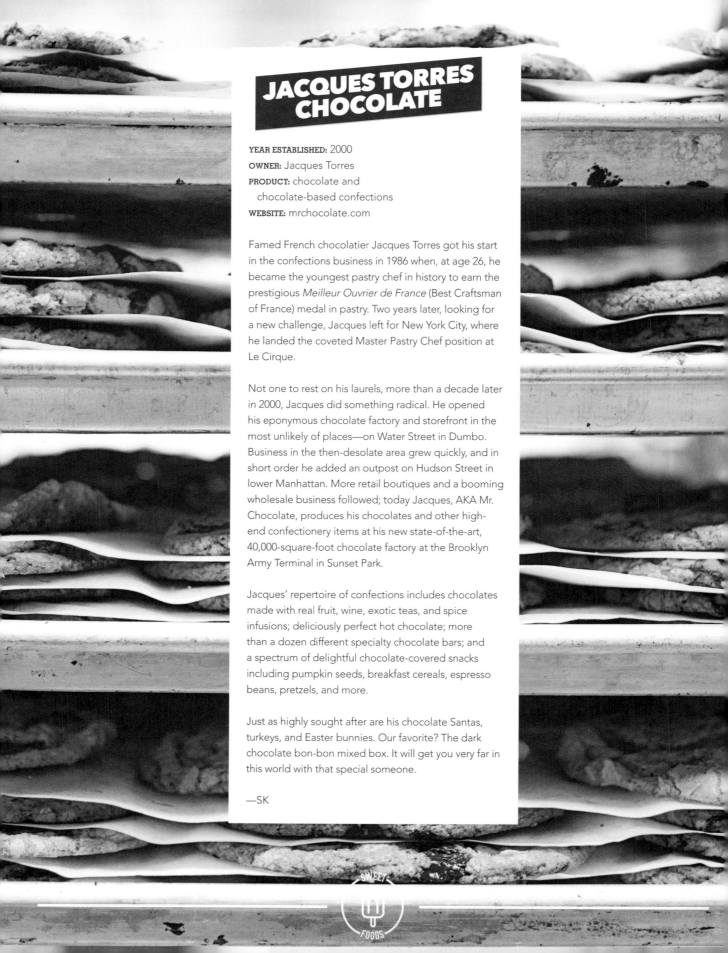

JACQUES TORRES CHOCOLATE

YEAR ESTABLISHED: 2000
OWNER: Jacques Torres
PRODUCT: chocolate and
   chocolate-based confections
WEBSITE: mrchocolate.com

Famed French chocolatier Jacques Torres got his start in the confections business in 1986 when, at age 26, he became the youngest pastry chef in history to earn the prestigious *Meilleur Ouvrier de France* (Best Craftsman of France) medal in pastry. Two years later, looking for a new challenge, Jacques left for New York City, where he landed the coveted Master Pastry Chef position at Le Cirque.

Not one to rest on his laurels, more than a decade later in 2000, Jacques did something radical. He opened his eponymous chocolate factory and storefront in the most unlikely of places—on Water Street in Dumbo. Business in the then-desolate area grew quickly, and in short order he added an outpost on Hudson Street in lower Manhattan. More retail boutiques and a booming wholesale business followed; today Jacques, AKA Mr. Chocolate, produces his chocolates and other high-end confectionery items at his new state-of-the-art, 40,000-square-foot chocolate factory at the Brooklyn Army Terminal in Sunset Park.

Jacques' repertoire of confections includes chocolates made with real fruit, wine, exotic teas, and spice infusions; deliciously perfect hot chocolate; more than a dozen different specialty chocolate bars; and a spectrum of delightful chocolate-covered snacks including pumpkin seeds, breakfast cereals, espresso beans, pretzels, and more.

Just as highly sought after are his chocolate Santas, turkeys, and Easter bunnies. Our favorite? The dark chocolate bon-bon mixed box. It will get you very far in this world with that special someone.

—SK

JOMART CHOCOLATES

YEAR ESTABLISHED: 1946; current store 1960
OWNER: Michael Rogak
PRODUCT: chocolates and confections
WEBSITE: jomartchocolates.com

Willy Wonka is alive and well in Brooklyn and his name is Michael Rogak, a third-generation Marine Park chocolate maker who calls himself the son of a son of a candy maker. He began working at his family store, JoMart Chocolates, at the age of 9—he was in charge of putting the eyes on chocolate Easter bunnies. After a stint as a special education teacher in the 1970s, Michael returned to JoMart and has worked 6 to 7 days a week ever since, hand dipping chocolate treats and other confections for generations of loyal customers.

JoMart has been on Avenue R since 1961 with the same sweet mission—to make the freshest and best chocolate around for generations of devoted customers. Hand painted chocolate Thanksgiving turkeys, rich butter crunch, and hand-dipped marshmallows—the store's bestseller—are just a few of my favorite things. Michael makes these and dozens of other melt-in-your-mouth confections, by hand, in the store's old-school chocolate factory. He uses his grandfather's copper kettles, and pours and cuts his confections on his father's marble table with his father's knives. You can taste the rich family history and handmade goodness in every bite.

Though customers hope nothing changes, Michael is always tinkering because it's what he loves to do. The day I visited, Michael was making a test batch of espresso bean toffee, a nut-free alternative to his more traditional peanut and almond brittles. The toffee was superb, with just the right amount of crunch and a rich espresso taste. Best advice I can offer: visit this old-school chocolate shop and taste for yourself. I guarantee you'll become a JoMart fan after just one bite.

—MSV

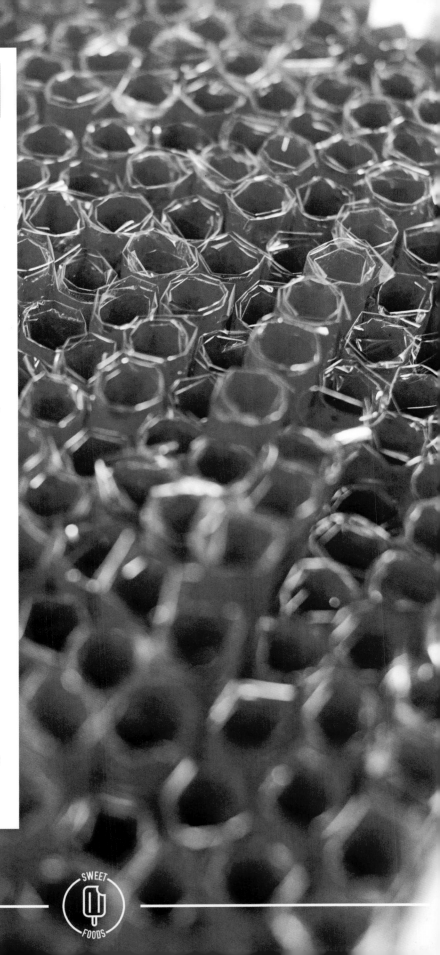

JORAY FRUIT ROLLS

YEAR ESTABLISHED: 1949
OWNER: Raymond Shalhoub
PRODUCT: fruit rolls
WEBSITE: joraycandy.com

Eating a Joray Fruit Roll is a walk down memory lane. One of my favorite treats as a child growing up in Queens, I was thrilled to learn they are still being made just blocks from where I now live. In an unmarked building on a residential street in Windsor Terrace, Raymond Shaloub is the master roll maker at the helm of the century-old company founded by his grandfather, Joseph.

Joseph's son Lou developed the recipe for fruit rolls, which were originally called "shoe leather" and inspired by a Lebanese confection of dried apricot paste. Lou and his wife pressed, dried, and rolled each by hand. Before packaging, stores would roll the shoe leather into cones and stack them in the window. Raymond nostalgically recalls how you never wanted to buy the bottom cone because that was the one that caught the flies!

Today, the pressing and rolling processes are mechanized—a handful of custom designed, one-of-a-kind machines press and roll the circles of real fruit into nine roll flavors, of which apricot is still the bestseller. Joray's Fruit Rolls are the only fruit rolls made in small batches from dried fruit (not concentrate—industrial sized sinks filled with bright orange dried Turkish apricots are proof), and slow dried (originally on clotheslines, now in two dry dehydrator rooms where the leather is laid out on racks). And they taste just as wonderful as I remember: fruity, sticky, and sweet. A childhood favorite lives on.

—MSV

SWEET FOODS

JOYVA

YEAR ESTABLISHED: 1907
OWNER: Richard Radutzky and Sandy Weiner
PRODUCT: halvah, tahini
WEBSITE: joyva.com

You probably didn't know there was a tahini pipeline in Brooklyn. Well, there is—and we found it! Literally running under Varick Street in East Williamsburg between two buildings owned by Joyva, the century-old confection company famous for its halvah, the pipeline brings tahini from their sesame seed processing facility to their halvah factory across the street.

Joyva tahini production dates back to 1907 when Nathan Radutzky, a Russian immigrant from Kiev, had an idea to make and sell halvah, the ancient Turkish sweet delicacy (*halvah* means "sweet meat") of ground sesame seeds, considered by many to be the Food of the Gods. He peddled it to Eastern European immigrants on the Lower East Side and it quickly became the confection of choice. Eventually, in 1910, Radutzky moved his business to Brooklyn, where it has remained ever since. Still family owned and operated by Nathan's grandsons, Richard Radutzky and Sandy Weiner, Joyva is the largest importer of sesame seeds in the country, bringing in 2 million pounds a year, and producing 20,000 pounds of halvah a day.

The recipe for making halvah begins with an extensive multi-day processing of the sesame seeds through the most wonderful old machines we've seen. The seeds are sorted, soaked, hulled, rinsed, dried, roasted, and ground into tahini, the base for the halvah. The tahini is then either packaged in its signature brown and orange tins or pumped to the halvah plant through the pipeline and poured into well-used old copper pots and combined with a taffy mixture of sugar, egg whites, and corn syrup. Then the time-honored tradition of hand kneading and stretching commences until sugary strands develop and the mixture becomes dough-like. The halvah is poured into molds, left overnight to harden, and cut into individual bars, often enrobed in chocolate and nuts.

Joyva also makes chocolate-covered jellies and marshmallow and sesame crunch candies, favorite holiday treats for generations.

—MSV

THE KALE FACTORY

YEAR ESTABLISHED: 2009
OWNER: Amy Hambury and Joe Orr
PRODUCT: kale chips
WEBSITE: thekalefactory.com

Shortly after the kale trend began to take the foodie world by storm in 2007, Joe Orr and Amy Hambury started making and selling kale chips at Joe's health food store on Flatbush Avenue. They introduced people to the wonders of this nutrient-dense, antioxidant-packed, vitamin- and fiber-rich super food, in the form of a snack. Some have called their raw, vegan, crispy kale leaves "Doritos for health nuts." I just call them addictively delicious.

Production has moved to The Kale Factory in Crown Heights, where they still make everything completely by hand. Locally grown, thick kale leaves are cut, washed, and spun dry, then laboriously massaged with a cheesy-tasting batter of nuts, spices, veggies, and lemon juice, and air-dried in a walk-in dehydrator for fifteen hours, thus preserving all the goodness kale has to offer.

The Kale Factory repertoire goes beyond chips, but stays true to its mission to make raw, kale-based foods. Try Greenola, granola with kale instead of grains, Kale Krackers, and Kale Powder and Kale Flakes, both great for smoothies.

—MSV

KBBK

YEAR ESTABLISHED: 2009
OWNER: Eric and Jessica Childs
PRODUCT: kombucha, SCOBY
WEBSITE: kombuchabrooklyn.com

If you're not familiar with the ancient tradition of kombucha, the fermented probiotic tea drink that has been touted as a magic elixir, Eric "Kombuchaman" Childs, owner of KBBK, will gladly walk you through the process and even set you up with everything you need to homebrew. Eric and his wife, Jessica, are the leading authorities on kombucha home brewing and SCOBY (Symbiotic Colony Of Bacteria and Yeast) farming. And their business is booming now that the detoxifying, energizing, immunity boosting, healing powers of kombucha have come to the attention of the mainstream.

Occupying the old packaging inspection lab at the Bed-Stuy Pfizer building, KBBK is covering all the bases. In their learning center, you can take a class on kombucha home brewing while sipping your choice of several kombuchas on tap from their 'Buch Bar. Go home with your own brew kit, which includes the freshest SCOBY (AKA mother) money can buy. And while you're there, grab their cookbook for ideas of how to cook with your SCOBY when her work is done.

Though their business once included 12-ounce bottles, Eric and Jessica have moved to a more sustainable model, offering only wholesale kegs for refill and reuse. So stop into dozens of markets, restaurants, and bars around NYC for KBBK fresh on tap and enjoy this nicely acidic, effervescent, sweet-tart treat. Your body and your mind will thank you.

—MSV

COFFEE, TEA
BEVERAGES

KINGS COUNTY DISTILLERY

YEAR ESTABLISHED: 2010
OWNER: Colin Spoelman and David Haskell
PRODUCT: bourbon, moonshine, whiskey
WEBSITE: kingscountydistillery.com

Kentucky-born Colin Spoelman and David Haskell make handcrafted moonshine, bourbon, and chocolate whiskey using a mix of traditional and contemporary techniques. The distillery uses premium grain, open-air fermentation, and pot distillation to make their spirits, aging them in a mix of barrel sizes.

Kings County's headquarters, the 115-year-old Paymaster Building in the Brooklyn Navy Yard, situated near the site of the great whiskey wars of the late 1860s in Vinegar Hill, looms large in the owners' approach and practice of their craft. They use organic corn from the Finger Lakes region of New York state and malted barley from the U.K., and employ traditional distilling equipment—most importantly their two copper pot stills built to their own specifications in Scotland—to make their distinctive whiskeys. Colin and David currently focus on three unique spirits: a "moonshine" (unaged corn whiskey); a young but surprisingly mature-tasting bourbon, their best-seller; and a popular (if somewhat disturbing to purists) chocolate whiskey, infused with ground cacao bean husks from Mast Brothers Chocolate (page 114) to give the concoction a robust, buttery, dark-chocolate flavor.

King County's moonshine and bourbon have both won "Best in Category" from the American Distilling Institute's Craft Spirits Awards, and the bourbon has won two silver medals from the American Craft Distillers Association.

Committed to using local materials and manufacturing in an earth-friendly way, Colin and David supplement their mash ingredients with corn and barley grown onsite next to their building at the Navy Yard, and the spent grain is recycled as compost and pig feed.

—MSV

ALCOHOLIC DRINKS

KINGS COUNTY DISTILLERY

BROOKLYN NAVY YARD

105

KRUMVILLE BAKE SHOP

YEAR ESTABLISHED: 2011
OWNER: Antonella Zangheri
PRODUCT: gluten-free baked goods
WEBSITE: krumvillebakeshop.com

Antonella Zangheri was diagnosed with celiac disease in 2009 and had to give up many of the foods she loved and had been eating since her childhood in the province of Emilia-Romagna, Italy. Disappointed with the gluten-free products available, she saw a need for more exciting options. She began baking them herself, and in 2011, established Krumville Bake Shop to share the gluten-free love.

Working from a light-filled kitchen in the Pfizer Building, Antonella creates delicious gluten-free focaccia, cookies, muffins, quiches, and specialty cakes that celebrate her rich Italian and Dutch culinary heritage. Using fresh, wholesome, non-GMO, preservative-free ingredients, Antonella is reinventing the way people think of gluten-free food. She works with whole grain flour blends like sorghum, brown rice, millet, and other ancient whole grains to achieve unique flavor and extraordinary texture in everything she bakes. I'm partial to her olive and pecorino focaccia and chocolate chip cookies, and want her gorgeous buttery lemon bundt cake at every brunch I host.

Antonella is capturing the attention of non gluten-free foodies, too, with her scrumptious creations. Mario Batali stopped by Smorgasburg one day and after tasting Krumville's Red Lady Chocolate Truffle Cake, exclaimed "Wow—it's amazing what they're doing without gluten these days. It's as good as anything with gluten…even better!" Music to Antonella's ears.

—MSV

SWEET SAVORY FOODS

LA NEWYORKINA

YEAR ESTABLISHED: 2010
OWNER: Fany Gerson
PRODUCT: Mexican ice pops and confections
WEBSITE: lanewyorkina.com

Fany Gerson, a graduate of the Culinary Institute of America, worked in a range of fine-dining kitchens around the world, including Akelare in Spain (three Michelin stars), and Eleven Madison Park in New York, before heading to her native Mexico to write a book about the wonderful recipes for sweets and frozen desserts she found there. Returning a year later, she began La Newyorkina, making paletas (Mexican ice-pops). Paletas, according to Fany, are to Mexicans what gelato is to Italians. The success of her first foray into selling the pops, at the Hester Street fair, prompted Fany to expand her business.

A few ice carts later, she opened a small baking factory with an adorable, tiny *tiendita* (shop) offering a line of old-fashioned Mexican confections that include heavenly puffed amaranth chocolate bites, deliciously spicy candied pepitas, Mexican wedding cookies called polvorones, as well as delightful coconut-lime candies and natural fruit gummies. Our favorite? The sumptuous morenitas (brownies with chipotle morita chiles, Oaxacan chocolate, and cajeta, a goat-milk caramel).

Everything at La Newyorkina is made from scratch using organic dairy products and the finest material—traditional Mexican ingredients such as tamarind, dried chilies, passion fruit, and hibiscus are imported from small producers in Mexico. Fany, now one of the most authoritative voices on Mexican confections, has a simple goal: to share the delicious sweetness and rich treats culture of Mexico.

—SK

LIDDABIT SWEETS

YEAR ESTABLISHED: 2009
OWNER: Liz Gutman and Jen King
PRODUCT: candy bars, caramels, caramel corn
WEBSITE: liddabitsweets.com

I can't think of anything better than handmade chocolate bars and caramels made with cupfuls of love and passion. That's what Liz Gutman and Jen King have achieved with Liddabit Sweets, darlings of the Brooklyn artisan candy scene. They are committed to producing small-batch candy bars, caramels, lollipops, caramel corn, honeycomb candy, and more, all by hand, all from scratch, and with the highest quality, locally sourced ingredients they can find.

Liz and Jen met in pastry school at the French Culinary Institute in 2007, and set out to make a superior candy bar. They took their first creations to the Brooklyn Flea in 2009, and what started as a side project born from a shared passion for responsibly made sweets quickly blossomed into a full-time venture with customers clamoring for more. They now have two retail locations, including their flagship store and kitchen at the Industry City Food Hall, and a cookbook, *The Liddabit Sweets Candy Cookbook*.

It's impossible to pick a favorite so you'll have to try all of Liddabit's whimsical confections—Sea Salt Caramels, Beer & Pretzel caramels (made with Brooklyn Brewery Beer), the King Candy Bar, and Bourbon Bacon Caramel Corn. Each bite invokes nostalgic childhood memories, but with more mature, sophisticated notes. Seriously, people, Liddabit Sweets are totally addictive.

—MSV

MAMA O'S PREMIUM KIMCHI

YEAR ESTABLISHED: 2007
OWNER: Kheedim Oh
PRODUCT: kimchi
WEBSITE: kimchirules.com

What do you do if you come from a family that emigrated from Korea and you love kimchi, but you profoundly dislike eating the version that your local deli has to offer, typically a syrupy kimchi full of MSG? You ask your mom for her kimchi recipe and experiment with it: all you need is ten tub-like buckets, some Napa cabbage, and time to ferment.

Kheedim Oh, who grew up in Maryland, was making a living as a club DJ when his kimchi-making took off. Now Mama O's offers not only a traditional-style kimchi but a number of other varieties. In addition to the classic Napa cabbage version, he also makes Baby Bok Choy Kimchi and Daikon Kimchi. And for those whose diets require avoiding fish sauce, there is the "Kosha" option, which is vegan. Brave souls will want to try the Super Spicy Kimchi made with ghost peppers. Mama O's also sells a line of kimchi pastes for making kimchi at home or just flavoring up your favorite dish. If you're really inspired by Kheedim's kimchi artistry, you might want to try it yourself with Mama O's Premium Homemade Kimchi Kit.

Kheedim also organizes the Kimchipalooza, an annual festival celebrating all things kim-chi, which allows Kheedim to indulge his two biggest passions: DJ-ing and kimchi. After all, he says, both "kimchi and DJing are just cutting and mixing!"

—SK

MAST BROTHERS

YEAR ESTABLISHED: 2007
OWNER: Michael and Rick Mast
PRODUCT: chocolate and chocolate brew
WEBSITE: mastbrothers.com

These bearded brothers are Brooklyn royalty. Rick and Michael Mast, the Iowa-born chocolatiers behind Mast Brothers Chocolate, first introduced us to "bean to bar," a whole new approach to chocolate. Their gorgeous packaging, meticulous process, exceptional design aesthetic, and of course, their uniquely delicious chocolate, has earned them a huge following and much respect in the artisanal chocolate world.

Mast Brothers' single original and blended dark chocolates are complex, slightly bitter, and acidic, but also rich and distinct. By adding only cane sugar to their chocolate, they are able to highlight the unique flavors and origins of the organic cacao beans sourced from small farms in places like Madagascar, Peru, and the Dominican Republic.

A visit to their industrial-chic factory in Williamsburg is a feast for your eyes and a treat for your taste buds. Their latest venture is a chocolate-centric brew bar where they offer brewed chocolate—a pour-over made with cacao nibs rather than coffee; cold-brew chocolate—steeped cocoa nibs that create an unsweetened drink similar to tea; chocolate soda; and chocolate milk. Rick and Michael can now be found across the pond as well, spreading Mast Brothers' love in London with their third chocolate factory.

—MSV

MITI MITI

YEAR ESTABLISHED: 2010

OWNER: George Constantinou
and Farid Ali Lancheros

PRODUCT: Columbian style dipping sauces

WEBSITE: mitimitifoods.com

Miti Miti is a popular Spanish saying that translates to "sharing half way" in English. A perfect name for the vibrant Columbian table sauces George Constantinou and Farid Ali Lancheros create in the kitchen of their popular Park Slope bistro Bogota Latina. Originally served exclusively in the restaurant with house-made plantain chips, customers began requesting them to go. Five years later, George and Farid, business and life partners, developed their sauce line, which now includes Green Aji, a vinegar based marinade bursting with parsley and cilantro; Chipotle Sauce, a smoky pungent mayo with chipotle peppers; and Red Aji Sauce, part salsa part vinaigrette with green, red bell, and chili peppers.

The men, married since 2011 and the parents of twins toddlers, Gustavo and Milena, have been recognized with numerous awards for their inclusive, community-based hiring and benefits practices, as well as their tireless campaigning with Freedom to Marry, an organization working to pass the Respect for Marriage Act.

The Miti Miti name now adorns George and Farid's latest venture, a tapas spot across the street from Bogota Latina, inspired by the sauce line and celebrating their diverse backgrounds—George is Costa Rican and Cypriot, Farid is Columbian and Palestinian. With the expansion of their pan-Latin culinary footprint, George and Farid are hard at work developing new recipes and growing their sauce line. That means more zesty goodness for us.

—MSV

SAVORY FOODS

GREEN AJI
TABLE SAUCE
Make your meal sing with
harmonious flavors imparted
from Latin America

...POTLE
...E SAUCE

S

Dip Sampler - $14.

Fritanga - $18.00
Coconut Shrimp $13.00
Fried Calamari $12.00
Empanada Sampler $15.00

Empanadas

Wheat:
    Shrimp - $5.50
    Beef - $4.00
    Guava - $4.00
    Goat Cheese - $4.50

Cornmeal:
gluten {Chicken - $4.00
free {Steak -
      {Domino-

MOMBUCHA

YEAR ESTABLISHED: 2009
OWNER: Rich Awn
PRODUCT: Kombucha concentrate
WEBSITE: mombucha.com

Brooklynite Rich Awn, founder of Mombucha, is a nano-brewer of flavored kombucha (for the uninitiated, kombucha is a fermented tea). Most store-bought kombuchas are diluted with water, but Mombucha is a concentrated kombucha. Rich's kombucha is "not pasteurized, not diluted," he says. "I use premium ingredients. I make it as my mom made it for me." Hence the company name: Rich's mom, convinced of its health benefits, brewed kombucha for her kids from the time they were very young. In 2005, after years of working in restaurant kitchens and in the advertising business, Rich found that his mom's passion and commitment had sparked his own interest, and he decided to give his own "mother culture" a try.

The quality and flavor of Mombucha comes from the essence of the steeped tea, herb, or root used in the brewing, and no flavoring is added after fermentation. Rich's most popular flavor is Gingermint, characterized by a burst of citrusy ginger flavor mellowed by sweetness from the mint. Mombucha's ingredients are sourced as locally as possible: the mint, for example, comes from the Eagle Street Rooftop farm just around the corner from Rich's little "brewing garage" at the northern edge of Greenpoint.

Gingermint has found a very loyal audience that Rich services by biking his liters of kombucha to his customers, but—get this—you can also taste it as a cocktail mixer at the Brooklyneer, a cocktail bar in Manhattan.

—SK

MORRIS KITCHEN

YEAR ESTABLISHED: 2009
OWNER: Kari Morris
PRODUCT: cocktail syrups
WEBSITE: morriskitchen.com

Morris Kitchen's flavored cocktail syrups began with a simple idea: "to share and create food." The idea was sparked by time Kari Morris spent in the south of France, where she was introduced to ginger syrup used in marinades, dressings, and drinks. Back in the States, she teamed up with her brother, Tyler, a NYC- based chef, bringing together her fine arts background and his culinary skills to create their first cocktail ginger syrup in 2009. They made 40 bottles with letter-pressed labels and sold them at a local Greenpoint market.

There are now five varieties of Morris Kitchen syrup and you will want to stock your bar and kitchen with every one—ginger (still the most popular), rhubarb, preserved lemon, spiced apple, and grenadine. They are all crafted from locally sourced ingredients like seasonal New York apples, rhubarb, and honey. Morris purees, juices, steeps, and preserves the fruit with salt and cane sugar so they can use local ingredients year-round.

Before Kari immersed herself in the food world, she was a fine arts major at California College of the Arts. Since she opened Morris Kitchen, painting has taken a back seat. But her well-trained eye and modern design aesthetic are evident in every aspect of Morris Kitchen, from the carefully chosen Pantone color palette of the bottle labels to the collaborations the company is doing with local artists, many of whom are Kari's former classmates. Illustrated recipe cards, ceramic cups, and hand dyed shibori napkins are just some of the artisanal items beautifully paired with Morris Kitchen syrups.

—MSV

NEW YORK DISTILLING COMPANY

YEAR ESTABLISHED: 2011
OWNER: Allen Katz, Tom Potter, Bill Potter
PRODUCT: gin, rye
WEBSITE: nydistilling.com

Allen Katz, cofounder of New York Distilling Company, began thinking about urban distilling more than a decade ago after a trip to Plymouth Gin in England. Several years later, a friend introduced him to Brooklyn Brewery founder Tom Potter, who had also been developing ideas about micro-distilling with his son, Bill. They made a perfect combination of expertise, as Tom knew how to build and grow a small business, and Allen is recognized as one of the top cocktail and spirits experts today. They decided to give it a go, set their sights on Brooklyn, and set up shop in a metal building on Leonard Street in Williamsburg.

Inspired by the historical styles of gin and whiskey, but also interested in making their spirits "purposefully different" yet still relevant, New York Distilling makes Perry's Tot Navy Strength Gin, the highest proof gin in existence today, clocking in at 144 proof. Their Dorothy Parker Gin is a more contemporary, fruit-forward option. Chief Gowanus New Netherland Gin, created by Dave Wondrich, cocktail historian and intro writer for this book, harks back to a recipe from an 1809 distilling manual. And Mr. Katz's Rock and Rye, popular in the 19th and early 20th century saloons and tempered with rock candy sugar, is New York Distilling's "fun, let your hair down" spirit, flavored with sour cherries, cinnamon, and orange peel. They also make Ragtime Rye, a straight rye whiskey, barrel-aged for two years.

Best of all, you can visit the distillery for free weekend tours. Then, thanks to their Farm Distillers License, saunter up to The Shanty, a saloon housed in the distillery, for a cocktail or a beer, and watch the stills work their magic.

—MSV

THE NOBLE EXPERIMENT

YEAR ESTABLISHED: 2012
OWNER: Bridget Firtle
PRODUCT: rum
WEBSITE: tnenyc.com, owneys.com

"Go big or go home." That's the motto Bridget Firtle lives by. She's the distiller, taster, bottler, operations manager, marketing, sales, and social media director at The Noble Experiment (TNE NYC), her small-batch, cane-to-glass micro-distillery in East Williamsburg. You get the picture. This one-woman artisanal maker is hardcore Brooklyn through and through, with a smart head on her shoulders (she was a hedge fund analyst before becoming a distiller) and a deep-rooted entrepreneurial drive handed down from generations of Brooklynites before her.

The Noble Experiment, housed in a brick building on Meadow Street, with a handsome tasting room in front and wood and glass-paned doors opening to this mostly industrial street, was the government's nickname for the 1919 Prohibition Act. But for Bridget, TNE NYC also refers to her "noble experiment, " jumping the Wall Street ship for something more tangible. With knowledge of the global spirits industry, she turned her eye homewards towards Brooklyn and set out to bring the art of rum distilling back to the USA.

Owney's Original New York City Rum is the product of her labor. The dry white rum is named after Owney Madden, a Prohibition-era rumrunner, bootlegger, and mobster who smuggled rum from the Caribbean to the U.S. via the shores of Rockaway Beach, Bridget's home turf. Made from three simple ingredients—molasses, yeast, and New York City water—Owney's Rum is smooth, pure, and perfect for an Owney's Original Mai Tai or Rum Negrowney.

—MSV

Own Yourself

the
NOB.
experim
nyc

TNE.NYC

NUNU CHOCOLATES

YEAR ESTABLISHED: 2007
OWNER: Justine Pringle and Andy Laird
PRODUCT: chocolate bars, ganaches, caramels
WEBSITE: nunuchocolates.com

Among the original group of food vendors selling their handmade fare at the first Brooklyn Flea back in 2008 was a husband-and-wife team who called their company Nunu Chocolates. Today, Nunu is a major player in the chocolate game, with two thriving Brooklyn retail locations.

It all started when musician Andy Laird and his wife Justine Pringle decided to make chocolates to put on the merch table alongside the band's CDs, shirts, and concert posters. Justine explains the company's unique name: "The term 'Nunu' is an affectionate nickname for little kids in Africa where I spent my childhood. My mother called me 'Nunu' while I was growing up and I've since heard it used as a term of endearment in many different countries and cultures. When Andy and I started Nunu Chocolates, it was with the belief that the world is a better place when chocolate is involved."

Now making handmade specialty chocolate bars, ganaches, caramels, and other delicious chocolatey treats has become a full-time job for Justine and Andy. Nunu uses a single origin cocoa bean derived from a Trintario and Criollo hybrid that is sourced from a sustainable, family-run farm in eastern Colombia. Justine shared the secret behind Nunu's delectable salt caramels—a touch of salt roasted into the caramel itself, which is then enrobed in dark chocolate, and sprinkled with Fleur de Sel…irresistible!

—SK

OMILK

YEAR ESTABLISHED: 2011
OWNER: Greg and Julie Van Ullen
PRODUCT: nut milks
WEBSITE: omilknyc.com

I'm a dairy devotee. Cow's milk and yogurt are what I crave day in and day out. But now that I've tasted OMilk, made from almonds and cashews, I'm totally hooked. Greg and Julie Van Ullen have created the first line of nut milks from pure, raw nuts treated with pressure instead of heat. The result is a dairy-free, protein-packed, smooth and delicious delight. And trust me, you don't have to be vegan or lactose intolerant to appreciate how good it is.

Greg and Julie began making nut milk as a hobby in a quest to eat healthier before their wedding. They taste-tested with friends, family, and coworkers, and everyone wanted more. Like so many others, they got their start at the Brooklyn Flea and sold 100 bottles their first day. Just the reinforcement they needed to turn their hobby into an artisanal mom-and-pop small business, now offering almond and cashew milks as well as cold-brew coffee milk, plus a few seasonal favorites, all preservative- and stabilizer-free.

Their process takes time but is well worth it. For their almond milk, they soak raw whole organic almonds from a small farm in California, remove the peels, then flash-blanch the nuts. Next, the almonds are blended with agave, sea salt, and water and the mixture is run through a hydraulic press before a final hand straining to remove any trace of pulp. But what sets this nut milk above the rest is that at no time is the milk heated, so the finished product is whiter, the flavor is purer, and the nutritional value remains intact.

—MSV

ONE GIRL COOKIES

One Girl Cookies is a beautiful narrative of refined aesthetics, family traditions, and a love for exquisite cookies.

The story starts when Dawn Casale left the glittery retail world of Barney's and retreated to her tiny kitchen in her fourth-floor walk-up to experiment with recipes, creating her now-signature, jewel-size cookies. In 2001, David Crofton, a bread baker and aspiring pastry chef, joined Dawn in her first professional kitchen and a few years later they opened One Girl Cookies' first shop just off Smith Street in Cobble Hill (and they married soon after). Here Dawn pays homage to her Sicilian family roots with a family tree mural of her vintage family photos, which also decorates their cookie boxes.

Among One Girl's many special touches are the girly names Dawn chose to christen her tiny treats; many of the cookies are named in homage to her favorite people, including Lucia, a layered cube

YEAR ESTABLISHED: 2000
OWNER: Dawn Casale and Dave Crofton
PRODUCT: baked goods
WEBSITE: onegirlcookies.com

of buttery shortbread and espresso-spiked homemade caramel glossed with bittersweet and white swirls of chocolate, which was named for her great-grandmother. Lana, a bittersweet chocolate sandwich filled with raspberry preserves, takes its named from Dawn's favorite high school teacher, who was a little bitter but mostly sweet.

One Girl Cookies' Cobble Hill shop and a second location in Dumbo are elegantly designed havens with a distinctive communal spirit, where you'll find Dawn showcasing her collection of gem-sized cookies on silver trays in a glass case, while her expanding line of layer cakes, cupcakes, and delicious whoopie pies are lovingly displayed on vintage porcelain cake stands. A pretty picture, indeed.

—SK

SWEET FOODS

OSLO COFFEE ROASTERS

YEAR ESTABLISHED: 2003
OWNER: JD and Kathy Merget
PRODUCT: coffee
WEBSITE: oslocoffee.com

JD and Kathy Merget opened their first coffee shop in 2003 on a bare and gritty industrial stretch of Roebling Street in Williamsburg. Naming their new shop Oslo in honor of Norway's exceptional and world-renowned coffee culture, they hoped to create a community gathering place for the neighborhood locals as well as a spot to grab a cup of well-brewed coffee. Three shops and a roastery later, Williamsburg's oldest coffee roaster is credited with helping to kick off the artisanal coffee scene in New York City.

They began roasting their own beans in 2007 in a garage space shared with other local artisans and craftspeople including a vintage motorcycle repair shop, a trapeze school, and a passel of woodworkers, painters, and machinists. This set-up exemplifies JD and Kathy's commitment to engaging and supporting their fellow local makers, where everyone is doing their own thing, yet benefiting and contributing to the fabric of the community.

Oslo roasts about 2,000 pounds of coffee a week, meticulously sourced from ecologically and socially sustainable farmers throughout Indonesia, Central and South America, and Africa. Their newly equipped Probat Roaster has a computerized component intended to modernize the process, but JD and his staff prefer to rely on their well-trained senses to ensure that their blends and single origin roasts—named for Norse gods including Thor, Odin, and Freya—maintain the handcrafted quality their customers have come to expect.

—MSV

OSLO
Coffee Roasters
Brooklyn, NY

OTHER HALF BREWING COMPANY

YEAR ESTABLISHED: 2013
OWNER: Samuel Richardson and
  Matthew Monahan
PRODUCT: craft beer
WEBSITE: otherhalfbrewing.com

Other Half Brewing is Brooklyn's newest craft brewery. It was founded in a small, run-down warehouse, where Carroll Gardens meets Red Hook, by Sam Richardson and Matthew Monahan, two former head brewers at Greenpoint Beer Works who set out to zap palates with out-of-this-world hoppiness, and are widely considered to be crafting the best IPAs in New York City.

Other Half Brewing's impressive lineup of 15 hop-prominent releases are West Coast-inspired, and include their signature Other Half IPA, the tropical-fruited Green Diamonds Imperial IPA, and their formidable Imperial Stout, a robust, chocolaty, and mega-hoppy brew.

Within a year of launching, Other Half became so popular that a number of its handcrafted ales and stouts are now permanent fixtures at many bars and beer halls across the city. Fans can also visit Other Half's tasting room located in a small annex off the main brewery.

Future projects include canning their IPAs, a huge financial commitment, and collaborations with other Brooklyn makers such as Van Brunt Still House (page 184), where the distillery's whiskey barrels will be used to age select batches.

Other Half is a new breed of brewer, one that produces beer one barrel at a time; if you manage to find one on tap, revel in your luck.

—SK

ALCOHOLIC DRINKS

135

OVENLY

YEAR ESTABLISHED: 2010
OWNER: Agatha Kulaga and Erin Patinkin
PRODUCT: baked goods
WEBSITE: oven.ly

Agatha Kulaga and Erin Patinkin met at a culinary-themed book club and bonded over their shared passion for food, drinks, and becoming entrepreneurs. They set out on a simple but noble mission—to create better bar snacks. Salty, spicy, sweet, comforting nibbles that complement cocktails and beer, like spicy bacon caramel corn and bacon-fat washed Old Bay peanuts. Bar patrons in Greenpoint and Williamsburg were happy—happy and craving more.

Agatha and Erin obliged and opened their storefront, Ovenly, a sweet, warm and welcoming place at the end of an industrial street half a block from the Greenpoint waterfront. Eager to connect with the community, they enlisted several local Brooklyn artisans to design the shop. I'm especially smitten with their lighting fixture created by brothers Evan and Oliver Halsegrave of hOme (they've done work for Mast Brothers (page 114) and Kings Country Distillery (page 104) too). But back to the sweets.

An antique glass case filled with freshly baked gluten-full, gluten-free, and vegan cookies, cakes, bars, and more, draws you in. Inspired by their Eastern European roots, Agatha and Erin continue to explore culinary traditions with their own fanciful and surprising twists.

I could sit at Ovenly from dawn 'til dusk. I'd need that long to eat though all my favorites, including Brooklyn blackout cake, salted chocolate chip cookies, and cheddar mustard scones.

—MSV

SWEET FOODS

P & H SODA COMPANY

YEAR ESTABLISHED: 2009
OWNER: Anton Nocito
PRODUCT: soda and cocktail syrups
WEBSITE: pandhsodaco.com

Brooklyn's artisanal makers movement is steeped in nostalgia. The drugstore soda fountain tops the fondest memories list, harking back to the days when soda jerks hand-mixed syrup and carbonated water to order. Anton Nocito, proprietor of P & H Soda Company, yearns to revive the fountain tradition. He handcrafts small batch all-natural soda syrups, in Greenpoint, that are perfect for making sodas (and cocktails) at home. All you need is a SodaStream or other carbonating gadget, and maybe a copy of his book, *Make Your Own Soda,* and you're good to go.

After years as a butcher and chef, Anton set out to open a sandwich shop featuring homemade sodas and ice cream. But once people at local markets tasted his custom made sodas—and Anton and his wife had a baby—the restaurant idea moved to the back burner and syrup took center stage.

He now makes six varieties year round for retail and restaurant clients—cream, ginger, grapefruit, hibiscus, lovage, and sarsaparilla, and a handful of seasonal flavors as well. With each sip, you are reminded that a trained chef is crafting these syrups. Each is a wonderful balance of not too sweet, not too dry, and slightly acidic, and all are bursting with fresh fruit, spices, and herbs.

—MSV

COFFEE, TEA & BEVERAGES

PELZER'S PRETZELS

YEAR ESTABLISHED: 2012
OWNER: Barella and Leon Pelzer Kirkland
PRODUCT: Philadelphia-style soft pretzels
WEBSITE: pelzerspretzels.com

I've had my fair share of NYC street cart pretzels, but have never liked them. Hard, dry, bready, and over salted, they're just not good. Barella Kirkland and Leon Pelzer Kirkland, owners of Pelzer's Pretzels, are on course to change that. Their artisanal soft pretzels are a tribute to Leon's hometown of Brotherly Love, and are made in the old-world style, hand twisted in the shape of a bowtie and given a lye bath for the perfect leathery crust and delicious, unique flavor.

Barella, formerly a beauty marketer, and Leon, a practicing attorney, are self-taught first-class pretzel makers. They set out to own their own business, not quite sure what that would be, and finally settled on pretzels to satisfy Leon's craving for a little Philly in Brooklyn. They began baking at home and selling at the now defunct Dekalb Market before being welcomed in to the Smorgasburg family. As their little business grew, they searched for a commercial kitchen and stumbled upon the perfect spot, a small take-out shop on a residential street in Crown Heights, just around the corner form where they lived.

They now bake hundreds of pretzels a day in a host of irresistible flavors, including Jalapeno Cheddar, The Everything, The Balboa (in honor of Philly's favorite boxer), and the Classic. These are so good, dare I say I'll never eat another NY pretzel again.

—MSV

SAVORY FOODS

PEOPLE'S POPS

YEAR ESTABLISHED: 2008
OWNER: Joel Horowitz, David Carrell, and Nathalie
  Jordi
PRODUCT: fruit pops, shaved ice
WEBSITE: peoplespops.com

People's Pops takes a classic icebox treat to
a whole new level. Trust me, you'll want to try
every one of these frozen delights, all made
from seasonal, fresh, local farmers' market fruits,
veggies, and herbs combined with other natural
treats such as yogurt and honey. With 100 flavors
in their repertoire, People's Pops offers an icy
treat for every taste, including out-of-the-box
combinations like Plum Shiso, Peach-Habanero,
and Pumpkin Pie with Whipped Coconut Cream.
Real fruit pops made for the people, by people!

Created by Nathalie Jordi, David Carrell, and Joel
Horowitz in 2008, People's Pops now has three
retail locations around NYC, a DIY-pop cookbook,
and stands at both Smorgasburg and the Brooklyn
Flea. Their sense of community is strong, and they
are committed to using ingredients from other
local Brooklyn food makers as well as working
with small local businesses—for example, they've
recently benefitted from the engineering skills of
Dave Liotti, proprietor of 61 Local in Cobble Hill,
who built their new-fangled pop stick stamper. It's
one gorgeous machine that saves them a whole
lot of time so they can focus on developing new
flavors.

People's Pops happily calls the Pfizer Building
home, where, in season, they make several
thousand pops a day. During our visit, we got
to taste a test pop—Carrot Apple Ginger with a
bit of cranberry thrown in for good measure—"a
veggie pop is a little crazy," you may say, but we
say, "No way!" Sweet and surprising, the flavors
are delicious and full-on—we bet you'll love it as
much as we did.

—MSV

PEOPLE'S POPS

BEDFORD-STUYVESANT

QUEEN ANN RAVIOLI & MACARONI

YEAR ESTABLISHED: 1972
OWNER: Alfredo Ferrara
PRODUCT: pasta, sauces, prepared foods
WEBSITE: queenannravioli.com

Alfredo Ferrara was 15 years old in 1955 when left his hometown of Bari, Italy, on the Adriatic coast, to find work in America. Five years later he returned to Italy, married his childhood sweetheart, Anna, and together they returned to the States where Alfredo installed and repaired pasta machines. But he dreamed of owning his own business and in 1972, that dream became a reality. He opened Queen Ann Ravioli & Macaroni in Bensonhurst and began making and selling gnocchi, slowly expanding the line to include fresh and dried pasta, ravioli, tortellini, stuffed shells, and manicotti.

Today, more than 40 years and three generations later, Queen Ann has remained a small, family-owned and operated business, now run by Alfredo's son-in-law, George Switzer. The 4,000-square-foot retail and factory space on 18th Avenue in Brooklyn's Little Italy houses the company's assortment of antique and updated machinery. They produce fresh pasta every day, gracefully churning out more than 30 varieties of the most perfectly plump and creamy stuffed ravioli, three sizes of ricotta impasta-filled tortellini, egg-batter crepes for hand-rolled manicotti, and a vast array of dried pasta. Sal mans the hydraulic pasta press, built more than a hundred years ago on the Lower East Side, while Frank prepares homemade sauces and dishes like eggplant rollatini and, my favorite, macaroni pie speckled with prosciutto.

Experimenting with progressive and modern flavors has kept Queen Ann competitive in today's market, but Alfredo, George, and their dedicated crew remain true to their methods of production, firmly rooted in the Old World techniques that make their pasta so quintessentially artisanal.

—MSV

6 GIANT GOURMET MANICOTTI

QUEEN MAJESTY

YEAR ESTABLISHED: 2013
OWNER: Erica Diehl
PRODUCT: hot sauce
WEBSITE: queenmajestyhotsauce.com

Erica Diehl grew up in Buffalo, New York eating chicken wings dipped in hot sauce. But the hot sauce was never quite hot enough. So, ten years ago, she began experimenting with her own recipes and in 2013, Diehl made it official, bottling two flavors of hot sauce under the name Queen Majesty, which also happens to be her DJ name. Erica's been collecting reggae vinyl for almost 20 years and spins Jamaican gems alongside classic tunes at gigs all over New York City. She believes the right music and the right food can enrich your soul.

Surrounded by vibrant yellow peppers, deep green jalapenos, and ripe orange habaneros, Queen Majesty is ready to get to work in the Red Hook kitchen she shares with other Brooklyn makers. Producing her hot sauce close to home (she lives nearby in Boerum Hill) keeps her connected to the community.

Though she's not a trained chef, Erica's passion for spice and her eye for design combine to help set her Scotch Bonnet & Ginger Hot Sauce and Jalapeño Tequila & Lime Hot Sauce apart from others on the market.

—MSV

RAWPOTHECARY

YEAR ESTABLISHED: 2012
OWNER: Stephanie Walczak
PRODUCT: raw complete nutrition juices
WEBSITE: raw-pothecary.com

"Drink to your health" is exactly what you'll do with Stephanie Walczak's line of fiber-rich blended juices. Her company is called Rawpothecary and each of her juices is designed to nurture your body, inside and out. Superfood ingredients like greens and seeds are blended with delicious organic fresh and dried fruit into flavorful and purposeful combinations that will give you loads of energy and leave your skin glowing like never before.

Stephanie, an art dealer and curator by trade, was juicing and experimenting with raw, organic, vegan, nut and dairy-free "drinkable food" for decades before she decided to turn her formula for nature's best medicine into a business. Hoping to change people's lives, with blends like Kalefonia Dreamin', Dandi Detox, and Cress Fresh, she has expanded the line to include terrific non-dairy alternatives like Sun Coffee and Mocha Chia made with hemp, chia, pumpkin, and sunflower seeds.

Kalefornia Dreamin' is one of my go-tos, packed with everyone's favorite green, kale, sweet bananas, blueberries, kiwi, and dates, and finished with coconut water for a perfect balance of herbaceous fruity goodness. Stephanie designs custom cleansing and detox programs, but I bet once you taste a Rawpothecary juice, you'll want them as part of your everyday routine.

—MSV

149

RED HOOK WINERY

YEAR ESTABLISHED: 2008
OWNER: Mark Snyder
PRODUCT: wine
WEBSITE: redhookwinery.com

Unbeknownst to most New Yorkers, Brooklyn once accommodated lush vineyards and a flourishing wine enterprise; almost two hundred years later, New York's almost-lost legacy of vinification is being salvaged by Red Hook Winery, the borough's only such effort.

Red Hook Winery founder Mark Snyder is dedicated to using grapes and wines exclusively from the three major wine growing regions in the state of New York: Long Island, Hudson Valley, and the Finger Lakes. And, says Mark, "We feel we are only really scratching the surface of the potential of New York as a very diverse region."

After touring the world for more than a decade with rock bands, Mark had visited vineyards all over the globe. Questioning why he couldn't find the small production wines he wanted to drink in New York, in 2008 he asked two Napa cult- winemaker friends, Abe Schoener and Bob Foley, to join him in a new enterprise. Red Hook Winery remains a small, handcrafted operation; even today the principals divide every lot of grapes in half so that each winemaker can experiment. Bob's wines tend to be more fruity and classic in style, while Abe's wines are redolent of of earth, metal, and fir.

They have made some 70 different wines, at home among Red Hook's eclectic assortment of restaurants and bars. Happily, Red Hook Winery survived the devastating damage caused by Hurricane Sandy and will continue to explore the potential of New York grapes.

—SK

ALCOHOLIC
DRINKS

REGAL VEGAN

YEAR ESTABLISHED: 2007
OWNER: Ella Nemcova
PRODUCT: vegan snacks
WEBSITE: regalvegan.com

Born in Latvia and raised in Brooklyn, Ella Nemcova has been cooking since she was seven. But she spent years in the advertising business before "running off with her first love—FOOD!" After a year of traveling and eating around the world, Ella returned to Brooklyn, and did a post-trip cleanse that transformed her body and recalibrated her way of eating and thinking about food.

Based on memories of the many international flavors she tasted during her time abroad, Ella started experimenting with vegan cooking, eager to make food that tasted amazing while also being wholesome and healthy. Her creative spirit led her to establish Regal Vegan, a boutique catering company, delivering delicious vegan meals throughout NYC. She also began making Faux Gras, her decadent and humane alternative to traditional duck liver foie gras. This rich and creamy blend of lentils, walnuts, caramelized onions, and miso was so darn good, vegans and carnivores alike were hooked.

Ella, dressed in a red chefs' coat to match her striking red locks, continues to handcraft Faux Gras along with her other small batch spreads; Basilicotta, a cashew-based, dairy-free ricotta, and Superfood Pesto, packed with kale, basil, and parsley. Staying true to her mission to make healthy, tasty food that's animal-free and planet-friendly, Regal Vegan's delicacies elevate vegan food to a whole new level of yumminess.

—MSV

ROBICELLI'S BAKERY

YEAR ESTABLISHED: 2009
OWNER: Matt and Allison Robicelli
PRODUCT: baked goods
WEBSITE: robicellis.com

Matt and Allison Robicelli didn't set out to become the king and queen of Brooklyn cupcakes. It kind of just happened. After a brief stint as owners of a Bay Ridge sandwich shop, they began offering baked goods, and word spread like wildfire about their delicious yet purposefully not-cute cupcakes. Truth be told, Allison never liked cupcakes; pie is her first love, with cookies a close second. But recognizing the appeal of a well-executed cupcake, they set out to make theirs about taste and flavor balance, and people got it. So Matt and Allison closed the shop and opened a wholesale bakery instead.

The Robicellis (they're husband and wife with two boys at home) both have extensive experience in the food business. Matt studied pastry at the French Culinary Institute and worked at City Bakery and Lutèce, among other places. Allison, too, is both a pastry and savory chef with catering and consulting experience. You can taste their combined talent and flair for baking in every bite of every cupcake (five bestselling flavors plus four seasonal flavors each month), brownie, whoopie pie, and cookie they make.

Both Matt and Allison grew up in Bay Ridge and never left. When they set their sights on opening a retail bakery in 2013, they looked no further than their home turf, reminding Brooklynites in the more gentrified neighborhoods that cool things were happening all over Brooklyn. And that's where you'll find these two, salt of the earth, funny, opinionated, hardworking, true-blue Brooklynites, day in and day out, baking, bantering, and connecting firsthand with the community they cherish.

—MSV

SWEET FOODS

Vegandoodles: $2.50

Chocolate Chip Cookies: $2

Coconut Cream Macaroons: $1

Oatmeal Raisin Cookies: $2

New Jersey Cookie: $2

Gingerdoodle Cookies: $2

Tres Leches

Brooklyn Blackout

Cinnamon Bun

155

SAHADI'S FINE FOODS, INC.

YEAR ESTABLISHED: 1999
OWNER: Patrick Whelan, Christine Whelan, and Ron Sahadi
PRODUCT: nuts and seeds
WEBSITE: sahadifinefoods.com

Way back in the 1890s, Abrahim Sahadi opened Middle Eastern food importer A. Sahadi & Co. on Washington Street in Manhattan. The business expanded when Abrahim's nephew, Wade, emigrated from Lebanon in the 1920s, and continued to flourish, providing olives, spices, tahini, and other Middle Eastern specialties to the growing Syrian and Lebanese communities. In 1948, the construction of the Brooklyn Battery Tunnel prompted Wade to purchase a building on Atlantic Avenue in Brooklyn, where he established the business that was to become Sahadi's Fine Foods.

Since then, this family business has grown into a specialty food retailer that still features Middle Eastern specialties (many homemade), and remains one of New York City's most important importers of nuts and seeds. Today Sahadi's Fine Foods is run by the third generation of Brooklyn-born and raised family members, who like to joke, "We were Brooklyn before Brooklyn was cool."

To accommodate their growing wholesale business, the family has recently built a modern manufacturing and distribution facility in Sunset Park, where they use the old-school Arabic-style method of dry-roasting pistachios, hazelnuts, and pumpkin seeds, and where they make their famous spice blend, zatar.

—SK

GRAINS OF PARADISE

BULK SHOP

CASHEWS
ROASTED SALTED
$7.75 LB

CASHEWS
ROASTED UNSALTED
$7.75 LB

PECANS
$8.95 LB

SALT OF THE EARTH BAKERY

YEAR ESTABLISHED: 2010
OWNER: Haskel Rabbani and Alexandra Joseph Rabbani
PRODUCT: baked goods
WEBSITE: saltoftheearthbakery.com

How Brooklyn is this for a mission statement? "To elevate the snacking experience." Alexandra Joseph Rabbani did just that in 2010 when she left her job in business development in order to dedicate her life to "re-imagining classic treats." The result: Salt of the Earth Bakery, where Alexandra curates selections of different sea salts from the south of France, sometimes with other exotic spices, and carefully infuses them into to her baked goods.

Salt of the Earth Bakery's signature is the Cookie, a decidedly adventurous take on the classic chocolate chip cookie: sweet and savory (thanks to the Maldon Sea Salt). The Heavenly Oat cookie unites chewy oatmeal with chocolate and Bali Rama Sea Salt. For brownie lovers, there's the Mayan, a power combo of chocolate, cinnamon, cayenne pepper, and Halen Mon sea salt. A fan favorite is The OMGCB (OMG Caramel Brownie), a mouth-watering onslaught of decadent chocolate brownie with rivers of handcrafted caramel, topped with French sea salt. How they get the caramel into the brownie is a tightly guarded secret!

Salt of the Earth Bakery cookies and brownies can be found in a slew of New York City shops, including Whole Foods and Fairway, and online through Amazon Fresh. Lofty sources indeed for an elevated snacking experience!

—SK

The Cookie
salt of earth
4 large cookies

The Chocoholic
salt of earth
4 large cookies

The Wild Oat
salt of earth
4 large cookies

The Kona

SALTY ROAD

YEAR ESTABLISHED: 2011
OWNER: Marisa Wu
PRODUCT: saltwater taffy
WEBSITE: thesaltyroad.com

Saltwater taffy is Brooklyn retro at its best. But the taffy I remember from trips to the boardwalk was overly sweet, artificially flavored, and never actually salty. Marisa Wu, the founder and confectioner of Salty Road, has changed all that. She makes the only small-batch artisanal saltwater taffy in New York City, flavored with herbs, spices, real fruit puree, and coarse sea salt.

After a decade in the film business, Marisa shifted gears and turned her attention to confections. She learned the business working at Liddabit Sweets (page 110) and was asked by a friend selling produce down at Rockaway Beach to try her hand at making saltwater taffy. Jen at Liddabit promptly dismissed the idea. Making taffy by hand was far too laborious, she said. But Marisa was intrigued and set out to see for herself. Experimenting with recipes and all natural ingredients, she hand pulled, cut, and wrapped her way to a flavorful, creamy, and unique sweet.

I visited the Salty Road candy factory just steps from the Brooklyn Navy Yard and felt like a kid in an old-fashioned candy store. From the classic taffy puller that aerates the mixture to the antique, 1940s Model K cutter and wrapper, this operation is a wonderful mix of the old and the new. Of course, my tour wasn't complete until I had tasted each one of Marisa's newfangled seaside treats. I do love them all, Salty Caramel Apple, Mango Lassi, and Salted Peanut, to name a few, but Bergamot is my favorite. It's surprisingly herbaceous (bergamot is the flavoring of Earl Gray tea), with just a bit of sweet and Marisa's signature salty crunch. A grown-up makeover for a nostalgic childhood treat.

—MSV

SALVATORE BKLYN

YEAR ESTABLISHED: 2007
OWNER: Betsy Devine
PRODUCT: whole milk ricotta
WEBSITE: salvatorebklyn.com

Salvatore Farina, proprietor of Enoteca Gustavo in San Gimignano, Italy, first introduced Betsy Devine to handmade ricotta. She came back to Brooklyn, began experimenting with cheese-making and soon, Salvatore Bklyn was born and named after the man who inspired her.

Betsy makes the most delectable small-batch ricotta I've ever tasted. Using the freshest and fattiest Hudson Valley whole milk, Salvatore Whole Milk Ricotta hangs super long to give it dense creamy texture, separating it from all other ricotta on the market. Betsy also makes Smoked Whole Milk Ricotta, cooked over the burning embers of sweet cherry wood.

Living and working in Brooklyn means a lot to Betsy. "Space to breathe, to dream. . .the feel, the energy, the people, and the sense that anything was possible" was clear from the get-go. Brooklyn continues to be a magical place for her to work and live, and she's committed to the borough. In March 2014, Salvatore Bklyn and three other Brooklyn makers moved to their own mini-factory in Red Hook. Betsy couldn't be happier, working among fellow food artisans in a neighborhood with the greatest sense of community she's seen in New York.

—MSV

SFOGLINI

YEAR ESTABLISHED: 2012
OWNER: Scott Ketchum and Steve Gonzales
PRODUCT: organic pasta
WEBSITE: sfoglini.com

Chef Steve Gonzalez and creative director Scott
Ketchum started Sfoglini in 2012 to supply
what they felt was lacking in New York City
restaurants: deliciously textured artisanal pasta.
What sets Sfoglini pastas apart is the makers'
innovative approach of incorporating non-
traditional ingredients while using traditional,
high-end tools in the production process. The
results are ingenious and delicious.

Steve uses traditional bronze dies in the
extrusion of fresh pasta, creating a textured,
porous surface, which allows the sauce to
cling to the pasta rather than sliding off and
slipping to the bottom of the serving dish. The
pasta is then air-dried at low temperatures for
several days to preserve its natural nutritional
components and lock in eyebrow-raising flavor.

Sfoglini's signature offerings include organic
durum semolina, whole-wheat, whole-grain,
rye, and buckwheat pastas. We particularly love
Sfoglini's line of seasonal pastas (beet, ramps,
chili pepper, cocoa, chestnut, mint, scallion,
nettles), each made with fresh, local ingredients
from New York City green markets and local
urban farms.

Sfoglini also partners with other food makers
to make innovative, original pastas, including
an Everything Bagel Fusilli made with spices
from BEYGL in Brooklyn; a collaboration with
the Bronx Brewery that uses the spent grain of
five different barley malts in the making of their
BxB Radiators; and a delicious Sauvignon Blanc
Reginetti, using the freshly harvested grape
skins of this varietal from Red Hook Winery
(page 150). Yum!

—SK

CUTTLEFISH SPACCATELLI

ZUCCA

16 OZ · 1 LB · 454 G

16 OZ · 1 LB · 454 G

SIXPOINT BREWERY

YEAR ESTABLISHED: 2004
OWNER: Shane C. Welch
PRODUCT: craft beer
WEBSITE: sixpoint.com

Sixpoint Brewery was founded in 2004 by Shane C. Welch, an avid home brewer hailing originally from Wisconsin. The company's name derives from a symbol that has been synonymous with the craft of brewing since at least the year 1300, when brewers adorned their barrels and breweries with a six-pointed star. The star symbolized the purity of the craft, and the six individual points each represented six different critical elements: grain, water, hops, yeast, malt, and the brewer. Sixpoint's signature symbol is a blend of the brewer's hexagram and the nautical star, a nod to Red Hook's industrial past.

It all started in a basement, where Shane took a "mad scientist" approach to the great American pastime of home brewing. Only ten years later, Shane's boutique brewery—now located in an 800-square-foot garage in Red Hook—produces 30,000 barrels of beer annually.

Sixpoint brews are wild and raw, showing that beer in its purest, most organic form is actually alive. Most of Sixpoint's draft beers are un-filtered, unpasteurized, and contain live active cultures. Many of their brews are made with locally sourced ingredients, including many items plucked from their brewery's own rooftop garden. Sixpoint rocks a highly experimental and innovative approach to "conceptual beer," which is how Shane describes Sweet Action, the brewery's flagship beer. "Is it a cream ale? Well, not really, because it is brewed with elements of a Hefe-Weizen. So it is a Hefe-Weizen, then, right? Well, no…because it has a hop profile similar to a Pale Ale. All right, well, what is it, then? It's something different altogether. It's Sweet Action. That's what it is."

—SK

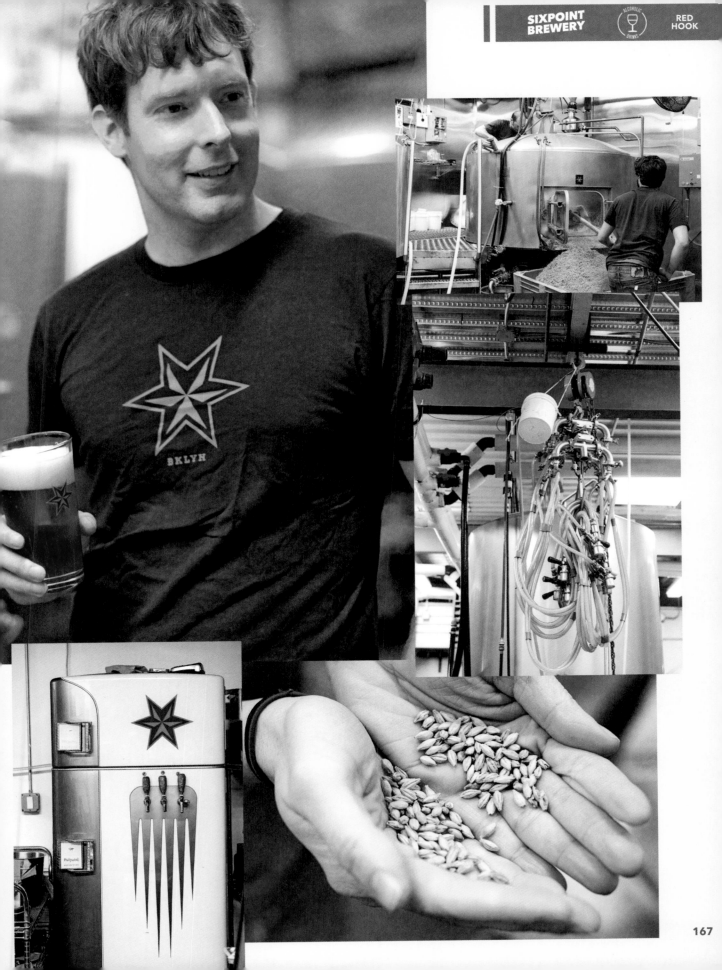

BKLYN

SOHHA SAVORY YOGURT

YEAR ESTABLISHED: 2013
OWNER: Angela and John Fout
PRODUCT: Lebanese yogurt
WEBSITE: sohhayogurt.net

Sohha means "health" in Arabic, and it's a perfect name for this wholesome Lebanese yogurt company. Owners Angela and John Fout are spreading the word that families can eat protein-rich yogurt made without sugar, thickeners, or preservatives, just like they make at home for their daughter, Savana. They handcraft their thick labneh-style yogurt in Sunset Park from a centuries old family recipe passed down to Angela from her mother, Wadad.

Three simple ingredients go into this exceptionally creamy treat: organic milk locally sourced from dairy farmer co-op Hudson Valley Fresh, live probiotic cultures, and sea salt. And they keep it simple, making only plain yogurt in two flavors: Original and Tangy. Keeping it plain allows their customers to eat it however they desire, topped with sweet fruit and honey, or savory, perhaps with cucumber, mint, and zatar. It's also wonderful to cook with and can be used as a substitute for mayonnaise or sour cream (Angela uses it for chicken salad). The possibilities are endless once you taste the creamy rich goodness of this yogurt.

Their company is young but growing fast thanks to the Fouts' passion for their product, their dedication to their mission, and the deliciousness of everything they make. Not to mention their boundless energy, as they travel daily between their Harlem home, their Brooklyn kitchen, and their shop in Chelsea Market, where they serve a host of Lebanese specialties, including, of course, fresh bowls of yogurt and whey lemonade, made from the probiotic byproduct of their straining process.

—MSV

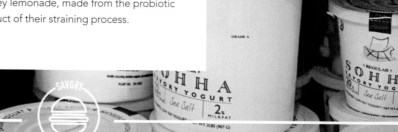

SPOONABLE

Michelle Lewis created Spoonable in 2011 after a career in the art world and a stint at the Modern Language Association (she speaks French, Japanese, and Chinese). One day, she made a cheesecake for a party, drizzled her homemade caramel sauce over it, and had a bit of sauce left over that she jarred and gave to friends as gifts. They went crazy for it and wanted more. Simple as that, Spoonable was born.

Michelle and her team now make five varieties of decadent confectionery caramel— Salty Caramel, Spicy Chili, Flowery Lavender, Chewy Sesame, and Buttery Apple Pecan—and one classic nostalgia-evoking butterscotch, Brooklyn Butterscotch.

YEAR ESTABLISHED: 2011
OWNER: Michelle Lewis
PRODUCT: caramel sauces
WEBSITE: spoonablellc.com

Her focus is on flavor and ingredient simplicity—sugar, heavy cream, unsalted European-style butter, and French sea salt. She uses no preservatives or additives.

The sweet, rich taste and super-smooth creamy texture are what make Spoonable's sauces excellent. What makes them exceptional is how well they pair with both sweet and savory foods—try them drizzled on ice cream, cake, or soft goat cheese; as a dip for fruit; or spread as a glaze on slow-cooked pork. Or try our own personal favorite way of enjoying this treat—on a spoon straight from the jar!

—MSV

SPOONABLE
BROOKLYN'S SAUCY CARAMEL
Spicy Chili
NET WT. 7.75oz (220 grams)

SPOONABLE
BROOKLYN'S SAUCY CARAMEL
Flowery Lavender
NET WT. 7.75oz (220 grams)

SPOONABLE
BROOKLYN'S SAUCY CARAMEL
Buttery Apple Pecan
NET WT. 7.75oz (220 grams)

PRONS
HEART
SPOON
♥ MOM

ANCHO
CAYENNE
PASSILA

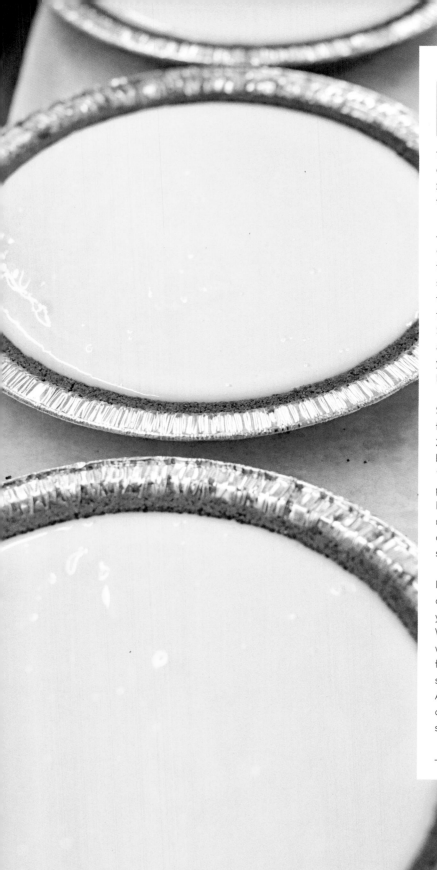

STEVE'S AUTHENTIC KEY LIME PIES

YEAR ESTABLISHED: 1994
OWNER: Steve Tarpin
PRODUCT: key lime pies
WEBSITE: stevesauthentic.com

Just after moving to Park Slope in 2002, I made one of my first Brooklyn foodie pilgrimages. Navigating the unfamiliar streets and piers of Red Hook, I went in search of Pier 41 and Steve's Authentic Key Lime Pies to share with friends and family at a rooftop party I was throwing that night. My expectations were high and Steve Tarpin's pies didn't disappoint. The crispy crust and dreamy sweet-tart custardy filling is all the proof you'll need that Steve's is the best, from Brooklyn to Key West.

Steve, a Miami native, has been selling his handmade five-ingredient key lime pies in Red Hook for more than 20 years. Now located on Pier 40, after Hurricane Sandy brought waist-high water into his original bakery, this "emperor of pie" has never wavered from his original purist mission: to make pies from fresh-squeezed key lime juice and handmade graham cracker crusts, with nothing from concentrate and nothing premade. This commitment is what sets Steve apart and makes his pies so heavenly.

It's nice to know that after all these years, little has changed: Although the bakery is larger, Steve still greets you at the small wooden counter surrounded by Key West memorabilia. A visit into the kitchen finds Steve's wife, Victoria, making Swingles, chocolate-enrobed frozen mini key lime pies on a stick, with their young son and daughter never far away. How lucky are they? And the lesson they are learning? That a healthy serving of hometown pride, tenacity, and integrity make for a sweet life.

—MSV

SWEET DELIVERANCE

YEAR ESTABLISHED: 2007
OWNER: Kelly Geary
PRODUCT: jams, spreads, butters, jellies, vinegars
WEBSITE: sweetdeliverancenyc.com

Kelly Geary is the chef-creator behind CSA-based, prepared food delivery service Sweet Deliverance, connecting farmers to consumers, and providing busy New Yorkers with expertly prepared wholesome food. Tired of the repetitiveness of restaurant life (she worked at Blue Hill at Stone Barns and Little Giant), Kelly creates a different menu each week based on what's coming from the CSA and delivers farm-fresh meals to her clients throughout New York City.

Her passionate support for local farms and her dedication to seasonal, responsibly sourced ingredients infuses everything Kelly makes. Not wanting to waste, Kelly began preserving and canning unused produce, crafting award winning jams, chutneys, butters, and more. She's even found time to write a cookbook, *Tart and Sweet: 101 Canning and Pickling Recipes for the Modern Kitchen*.

Kelly's kitchen is a bit off the beaten path, beside the BMT Canarsie Line on Atlantic Avenue. While her windows look out onto a quintessential Brooklyn landscape, the walls inside are lined with jars of preserved organic Meyer lemons, glass jugs of fermented sodas, and ceramic tubs of elderberry vinegar, reminding us that the local, small-batch, artisanal movement is alive and well even in the midst of our great urban jungle.

—MSV

THE WHITE MOUSTACHE

The story behind The White Moustache, a yogurt company based in Red Hook, is nothing short of inspiring. Whip-smart and determined beyond compare, founder Homa Dashtaki began making and selling her family's Iranian strained yogurt at farmers' markets in California. But the health department shut her down over archaic pasteurization regulations. Homa, a lawyer by trade, fought back, but to no avail. Obstacles continued to arise, yet Homa's obsession with yogurt making grew.

Fast forward to a fortuitous trip to Brooklyn. Homa saw her friend Betsy Devine (page 162) who was blown away by what Homa was making. The rest is a testament to the strength of the bonds in the artisan community. Betsy invited Homa to share her kitchen and Homa never left. The little factory on Commerce Street organically became an incubator of sorts and gave a talented maker a home. As Homa likes to say, the "real and…authentic" artisanal food scene in Brooklyn gets it, without compromise, and that's why she gets to do what she loves.

YEAR ESTABLISHED: 2011 started in California; 2013 moved to Brooklyn
OWNER: Homa Dashtaki
PRODUCT: Iranian and Greek style yogurt
WEBSITE: thewhitemoustache.com

Homa's pride in her product and exuberant pleasure in my reaction to each delicious taste is honest and abundant. White Moustache is a rising star in a market saturated with yogurt options. Packaged in adorable glass jars with black and white tops adorned with the white moustache logo, Homa's ultra creamy, rich, luxurious yogurt is made from just two simple ingredients, Hudson Valley Fresh organic milk and active live probiotic cultures. Each batch is coddled under blankets for optimal culturing, then hand-strained.

The Persian style is saucy and perfect for eating sweet or savory. Moosir, yogurt mixed with Iranian leopoldia shallots, is the artisanal answer to onion dip. Homa's Greek yogurt is thicker, and blended in mouthwatering varieties reminiscent of flavors from Homa's Iranian heritage like Sour Cherries, Sweet Beets, and a traditional preparation with raisins, mint, and walnuts called Yalda. She also sells the probiotic byproduct whey, perfect for smoothies, brining, or straight up.

—MSV

SWEET FOODS

the
WHITE
MOUSTACHE

Whey
Fresh & Pure

Perfect for
smoothies, raw soups,
sauces, cocktails and
post-workout hydration.

An excellent source of live
probiotics and calcium.

1 Liter (34oz)

SMALL BATCH · OLD WORLD

TUMBADOR CHOCOLATE

YEAR ESTABLISHED: 2006
OWNER: Jean-François Bonnet, Michael Altman
PRODUCT: chocolates and confections
WEBSITE: tumbadorchocolate.com

Jean-François Bonnet knows a thing or two about chocolate. He trained under a Michelin two-star chef in France, before coming to the U.S. to work as a pastry chef in some of New York's finest restaurants. Now as the executive chef at Tumbador Chocolate in Sunset Park, Jean-François creates luxurious chocolate confections for private-label clients like Barclays Center and Murray's Cheese, and five-star hotels throughout the country.

Though private label is their primary business, lucky for us, Tumbador also offers a full line of chocolate treats available at markets throughout New York. My favorites are the Lil' Devils (a far more delicious take on the Ring Dings of my youth) and PB & J bars, nostalgic treats that taste like good old-fashioned American childhood. That said, after a visit to their Industry City factory and my fair share of bonbons and chocolate-enrobed caramel, I'd happily eat any one of Jean-François' creations.

Tumbador is named for the worker on a cocoa plantation who shakes and listens to the cocoa pods to make sure they are ready to pick, an apt name for a company that prides itself on using exceptional techniques and the highest quality ingredients. No short cuts here. Chocolate from E. Guittard, tempered for just the right texture and shine; ethically sourced fruits, nuts, and spices; hand packaging; and all printing done in-house for a totally responsibly product.

Combine this with Jean-François' impeccable taste and technique, and each bite of Tumbador chocolate is a sumptuous delight.

—MSV

UNCOUTH VERMOUTH

YEAR ESTABLISHED: 2012
OWNER: Bianca Miraglia
PRODUCT: vermouth
WEBSITE: uncouthvermouth.com

Vermouth, once an uninspiring fortified wine relegated to the back of the liquor cabinet, is getting a modern artisanal makeover, earning its place among the best craft spirits being made today. With no particular recipe or regulations required, Bianca Miraglia, owner of Red Hook-based Uncouth Vermouth, spends her days meticulously crafting seasonal vermouths that are delightfully surprising and full of fresh, herbaceous flavor.

Uncouth Vermouth is the ultimate one-woman operation. Bianca spends her days, with her dog Emmett as her only company, at her distillery and tasting room (open by luck or appointment only). Housed in a former biker billiard bar, her space is now distinctly more feminine and adorned with Miraglia family photos and memorabilia, as well as artwork by the French collagist Matthew Prose that Inspires her to work hard and think outside the box.

Bianca had worked in the wine industry for more than a decade, but her fascination with vermouth began while she was staging quirky pop-up cocktail parties. Not into the commercial syrupy-sweet varieties, Bianca began experimenting with steeping fresh delicious wine from Red Hook Winery with locally foraged or farm-sourced herbs, barks, roots, and fruits. Fortified with New York State grape brandy ("the real shit") and relying only on residual sugars as sweeteners, Bianca's result is a balanced, naturally sweet, but not cloying, dry and slightly bitter vermouth that's appealing to the informed modern palate. Rest assured, what's inside each bottle bears no relation to the silhouetted logo of an uncouth Victorian-era woman with her finger up her nose.

—MSV

UNION ST. HONEY

YEAR ESTABLISHED: 2012
OWNER: Jon and Jaxon Derow
PRODUCT: honey

Jon and Jaxon Derow's story is short and sweet. Jon, a full-time art conservator, was looking for an engaging way to stay connected with his teenage son, Jaxon. After having taken a beekeeping class—a huge trend in Brooklyn in the past few years since bee keeping became legal in New York City in 2010—he purchased three hives.

The Derows now have two hives on the rooftop of their house on Union Street, and one hive in a garden nearby. While the concrete jungle of Brooklyn isn't the friendliest place for agribusiness, both Prospect Park and the Brooklyn Botanic Garden boast numerous flowering trees that are treated with fewer pesticides than in rural areas. It all adds up to a surprisingly welcoming environment for honeybees that, in kind, help maintain the health of the city's ecosystem and provide us with a sweet reward.

Jon and Jaxon are now in their third year of making honey, and have three harvests per year, in July, August, and October. 2014 was their most productive year to date, with enough honey to fill 600 jars of their flavorful and fruity-tasting raw honey (meaning minimally filtered, unheated, and unprocessed).

Reflecting on his unusual approach to bonding with his son, Jon says, "Beekeeping is fun but challenging, and the honey is just a bonus." Hooray for father-son bonding, which led to this rich, dark, and flavorful harvest made by Brooklyn bees.

—SK

VAN BRUNT STILLHOUSE

YEAR ESTABLISHED: 2012

OWNER: Daric Schlesselman and Sarah Ludington

PRODUCT: rum, whiskey, rye, grappa, moonshine

WEBSITE: vanbruntstillhouse.com

Daric Schlesselman comes from a long line of Wisconsin farmers, and his connection to the land is reflected in his passion for cooking and gardening. His former career in television, most recently as an editor on *The Daily Show*, while fun and rewarding, didn't offer the everyday tactile rewards Daric was craving. So when he and his wife Sarah Ludington began brainstorming about business ideas, they quickly decided on Daric's home brewing hobby. They jumped on the artisanal spirits bandwagon and got to work renovating an old Red Hook paint factory, now home to Van Brunt Stillhouse.

Named for the early Breukelen farmer, Cornelius Van Brunt, Daric and Sarah's distillery makes rum, bourbon, rye, whiskey, grappa, and moonshine from New York State corn, wheat, and rye, and malted barley that's sourced from around the world. Their custom-built German still is the heart of the operation and shifts easily from one spirit to another, while keeping the aromatic qualities intact. And their preference for miniature barrels increases the amount of flavor the liquid absorbs from the wood and allows them to age their whiskey at a more robust rate.

Daric and Sarah love coming to work every day in a neighborhood they call "magical" for its creative nature and proximity to the water, which provides them with wonderful light and a nice maritime breeze. Their sun-drenched, in-house tasting room is the perfect spot to take it all in and enjoy the fruits of their labor.

—MSV

VAN LEEUWEN ARTISAN ICE CREAM

YEAR ESTABLISHED: 2008

OWNER: Ben Van Leeuwen, Laura O'Neill, Pete Van Leeuwen

PRODUCT: ice cream

WEBSITE: vanleeuwenicecream.com

This story starts with Ben Van Leeuwen, whose college career was funded by his job driving an ice cream truck. Having gotten to know the business, Ben soon decided he'd like to have an ice cream truck of his own, one that offered exceptionally good-tasting ice cream. In 2008 he, his brother Pete, and their Australian friend Laura O'Neill hit the road with their first two distinctively butter-yellow 1950s-style ice cream trucks. A year later Whole Foods contracted to start carrying their ice cream in pints, and now Van Leeuwen owns and operates six trucks in Brooklyn and LA, and four stores in Brooklyn and in Manhattan.

Van Leeuwen's Ice Cream is made in Greenpoint, Brooklyn, according to simple, traditional methods—using fresh milk and cream that is hormone- and antibiotic-free, cane sugar, egg yolks, top-quality fruits, chocolates, spices, and nuts sourced from small producers. As Ben points out: "Not all of our ingredients are certified organic, but they are all exactly what they say they are. Strawberry is strawberry. Pistachios are pistachios."

Continuing to innovate, the Van Leeuwen trio has developed a delicious vegan ice cream made from coconut and cashew milk, raw cocoa butter, virgin coconut oil, and organic sugar cane—a frozen treat that eschews thickeners, stabilizers, and gums in favor of natural ingredients and a purely decadent result.

—SK

PROUDLY SERVING LOCALLY ROASTED TOBY'S ESTATE

VAN LEEUWEN coffee!

BREWED COFFEE	sm $1.75 · med $2.25 · lg $2.75
COLD BREW ICED COFFEE	$3.50
ESPRESSO or AMERICANO	$2.75
LATTÉ	hot $4.25 / iced $4.75
CAPPUCCINO	$3.75
CORTADO	$3.50
MACCHIATO	$3.25
MOCHA LATTÉ	$5.25 / iced $5.75
CHAI TEA LATTÉ	$4.00 / iced $4.50
"dirty" CHAI LATTÉ	$5.00 / iced $5.50
HOT CHOCOLATE	$4.50
HOT TEA (loose-leaf & organic)	$2.50
ICED TEA (ask us today's flavor!)	$3.00

AFFOGATO
a double shot
of espresso over
ice cream $5.50

COLD BREW FLOAT
iced coffee with
a scoop ice cream!
$7.

substitute
SOY or ALMOND
"milk" 25¢

extra
ESPRESSO SHOT $1.00

WHIMSY & SPICE

YEAR ESTABLISHED: 2008
OWNER: Mark Sopchak and Jenna Park
PRODUCT: baked goods, marshmallows, hot chocolate mixes
WEBSITE: whimsyandspice.com

"I'm thinking about homemade marshmallows," my friend Mark Sopchak said to me in February 2008. "Brilliant idea," I replied. After tasting my way through batches and batches of delicious squares of confectionery heaven, I knew he was onto something. Just two months later, Mark and his wife Jenna Park founded Whimsy & Spice in Park Slope and debuted their line of artisanal marshmallows and other "sweets with a dash of spice" at the first ever Brooklyn Flea.

Mark is a pastry chef extraordinaire who brings a lifetime of fascination with Asian and African spices to everything he bakes. His homemade spice blends, like curry powder and garam masala, add distinctive savory flavors to his sweet treats. Jenna, an award-winning graphic designer and art director, brings her smart, modern design sensibility to the lovely packaging and mouth-watering photography for all the Whimsy & Spice products.

Honey lavender shortbread, massaman peanut butter sandwich cookies, and chocolate stout marshmallows are just a few of my favorites. You can still find Mark on Saturdays at the Flea, sometimes assisted by his daughters, ready with a handmade treat and a smile.

—MSV

whimsy&spice

Earl Grey
HOT CHOCOLATE MIX

WHISK 3 TABLESPOONS OF MIX INTO
1 CUP OF STEAMING HOT MILK

whimsy&spice

Earl Grey
HOT CHOCOLATE MIX

WHISK 3 TABLESPOONS OF MIX INTO
1 CUP OF STEAMING HOT MILK

WIDOW JANE

YEAR ESTABLISHED: 2012
OWNER: Daniel Prieto Preston
PRODUCT: bourbon whiskey
WEBSITE: widowjane.com

One sip of the uniquely rich Widow Jane Heirloom Bourbon Whiskey, and you know that this is a spirit made with a very specific vision. Daniel Preston, who also owns Cacao Prieto (page 48) started by purchasing a historic Upstate New York limestone mine with the rather startling name of Widow Jane. The mine was known for its Rosendale limestone, which possesses an even higher ratio of beneficial minerals than that typically found in Kentucky (the traditional locale of bourbon-makers), and its sparkling waters are now used to distill all the artisan spirits Prieto makes in Red Hook.

Daniel had two goals in making his bourbon: he wanted to expand upon the palate of even the most vaunted bourbons and to make a product that would be 100% GMO free, from the enzymes used in the fermentation to the grains used in the mash. So he undertook the unusual and costly step of growing his own corn in the Hudson Valley, using two heritage varieties with the whimsical names of Wapsie Valley and Bloody Butcher.

After the harvest his corn is brought to Red Hook where it is milled, fermented, and pot-distilled at the Cacao Prieto distilling facility, and then aged for about a year in oak barrels across the street from the factory.

—SK

WIDOW JANE
Small Batch Whiskey · Brooklyn

WIDOW JANE
Artisan Batch Whiskey · Red Hook, Brooklyn

CONDIMENTS

Brooklyn's makers are rethinking classic condiments and inventing new ones. Sriracha mayo, probiotic hot sauce, and Indian-style relish share shelf space with updated versions of ketchup and mustard. These are a few of our newfangled favorites.

Empire Mayonnaise is a far cry from the ubiquitous Hellman's variety: Elizabeth Valleau and Sam Mason have taken this simple, everyday spread to a whole new level, creating all-natural, small-batch, and exotically flavored mayonnaise with mouth-watering names such as White Truffle, Bacon, Sriracha, and Lime Pickle, all made from non-GMO oils and the freshest cage-free and pasture-raised eggs.

Tin Disdarevic has started a mustard revolution, creating a simple, natural wholegrain mustard, as well as a smoother, spicier variety. **Tin Mustard's** texture is really what makes this condiment shine in an array of dishes.

Family owned and operated since 1964, **Michael's of Brooklyn** produces six different kinds of classic tomato sauces based on generations-old family recipes. Their restaurant and adjacent retail shop have been Brooklyn institutions for nearly half a century.

Sonya Samuel's **Bacchanal Sauce** is an island vacation in a bottle. A fiery-hot pepper sauce bursting with all-natural, exotic, tropical flavor capturing the tastes, excitement, and revelry of a Caribbean party. A unique combination of spicy, tangy, and sweet.

Sunny Bang Private Label makes a probiotic hot sauce from four simple ingredients, through natural lactic fermentation: Red Holland chile peppers, Maine sea salt, white wine vinegar made by a Benedictine nun in Upstate New York, and filtered NYC tap water. Their fresh-tasting and pleasantly-hot sauce has no additives, preservatives, or added sugars, thus accentuating and enhancing any dish with vinegar-driven, mind-numbing heat without masking the flavors.

Joshua Sharkey of **Bark NYC** makes a variety of house-made condiments, notably the unique tasting Bark Relish, which is sweet, tangy, with a touch of heat from mustard seeds and a little cayenne pepper, and cuts through all the rich, meaty, fatty, smoky flavor of everything from Bratwurst to Weisswurst and Bark's Classic Pork and Beef Weiners.

EMPIRE MAYONNAISE
TIN MUSTARD
MICHAEL'S OF BROOKLYN
BACCHANAL SAUCE
SUNNY BANG PRIVATE LABEL
BARK NYC
BROOKLYN DEHLI
SAUCY BY NATURE

Chitra Agrawal started producing her own achaars as most of the ones sold in shops were too salt-heavy, full of preservatives, and just didn't taste homemade. **Brooklyn Dehli's** achaar, an Indian relish sometimes referred to as "Indian pickle" is made from local, seasonal fruits and vegetables, spices, chilies, and oil. It's spicy, sour, sweet, and savory in flavor and can be used as a condiment or as a base when cooking. She likes to experiment with local produce like rhubarb and American gooseberries that are not found in traditional Indian recipes.

Caterer extraordinaire Przemek Adolf created **Saucy by Nature** BBQ sauce with his longtime friend Monika Luczak after years of traveling together and tasting exotic sauces and spices. Using locally sourced ingredients and fair-trade coffee, their sauce is rich and tangy with hints of molasses and a touch of heat. It's the perfect addition to any urban rooftop barbecue.

SWEETS & TREATS

Homemade sweets are at the heart of the artisanal food movement, a nostalgic walk down a memory lane that is lined with buttery biscuits, fresh-baked bread, flaky pies, and handcrafted chocolates. These indulgences transport us back to childhood when simple treats meant so much. Here's a taste of a few more of Brooklyn's best.

Ryan Cheney of Red Hook's **RAAKA** and head chocolatier Nate Hodge, specialize in organic, bean-to-bar, virgin or "low-temperature" chocolate. They don't roast their cocoa beans, so as to avoid destroying the original flavor; instead RAAKA "massages" and ferments the beans into dark and flavorful chocolate, replicating the handmade Thai cocoa truffles that first inspired Ryan.

Hana Pastries, a gluten-free bakery in Sunset Park, also found inspiration in Asia. Owner Nicole Bermesolo and chef Michael Hu take favorites like cupcakes, muffins, and brownies, and reinterpret them by adding Japanese flavors to create treats like Miso Brownies and Green Tea Muffins.

Brooklyn Biscuit baker Elizabeth Santiso took up the challenge to be "a Yankee makin' the best biscuits in the North—hands down." So expect classic flaky and fluffy biscuits with a twist, in her signature Vermont Cheddar & Jalapeno Biscuits, Savory Mushroom & Shallot Biscuits, and Sun-Dried Tomato, Parmesan & Fresh Rosemary Biscuit.

Greenpoint's **Pie Corps** is where "pie-oneers" Cheryl Perry and Felipa Lopez are making life a bit tastier, baking savory and sweet seasonal pies—Apple Crumb with Rosemary Caramel and Honey Lavender Custard with Sea Salt Crumb Crust—are standouts. And don't miss their medallion-sized pie pops with apple or chocolate filling.

Sisters Ali Borowick Zmishlany and Lauren Borowick of **Fatty Sundays** make chocolate-covered pretzel sticks in fun flavors like PB & J, toffee, and spicy almond. Growing up in a health-conscious family, Sunday was the only day when the sisters were allowed to indulge—now every day is Sunday for these two.

Known for artisan breads like a hearty wheat loaf with bourbon-soaked currants, raisins, and toasted pecans, and scrumptious sandwiches sold daily from a takeout window in Bed-Stuy, **SCRATCHbread** owner Matthew Tilden also churns out sweet fare like Pecan Sticky Buns and delectable Buttercream Brownies.

RAAKA
HANA PASTRIES
BROOKLYN BISCUIT
PIE CORPS
FATTY SUNDAYS
SCRATCHBREAD
BROOKLYN BELL
MONSIEUR SINGH

Couple Ron and Kate Cunningham run the busy scoop shop **Brooklyn Bell**'s The Local in Crown Heights, where Ron produces all-natural, traditional American ice cream. Kate makes Good Bars, which are delicious handmade granola bars that happen to be vegan and are packed with super foods and bold flavors.

Lassi, a 5,000-year-old yogurt, fruit, and spice drink, was conceived as part of ayurveda, India's practice of holistic medicine and wellness. Combining ancient goodness with a delicious modern twist, Karan Gera of **Monsieur Singh** pedals his frozen lassie push-up pops, in flavors like mango mint ginger and honey lemon spearmint, on his bicycle-drawn pop cart emblazoned with the tagline, "Endorsed daily by a billion Indians."

ERIC DEMBY AND JONATHAN BUTLER

The Brooklyn brand is alive and well not only in Brooklyn, but around the globe. People travel over oceans and continents to come to New York in search of the Brooklyn energy. It's known as that fabled place where you go to follow your passion, and you can create, build, and be anything.

The Brooklyn Flea serves as an incubator for Brooklyn-made brands. It perfectly captures this sense of opportunity, combining the powerful draw of Brooklyn with the enormous potential for artisanal food and home goods makers to capitalize on the growing yearning for handmade products and simpler ways. But when Eric Demby and Jonathan Butler decided to create the Brooklyn Flea in a schoolyard in Fort Green in the spring of 2008, they just wanted to capture what they felt separated Brooklyn from everywhere else.

Timing was everything. An awareness of "Brooklyn Made" was beginning to stir beyond our borders and Eric and Jonathan were uniquely positioned to ride that wave. Eric worked as communications director and speechwriter for former borough president, and number-one Brooklyn cheerleader, Marty Markowitz. And Jonathan had launched Brownstoner, a "New Brooklyn" real estate blog, in 2003. They recognized the changing landscape of the borough and wanted the Flea to be an authentic experience, a market where locals and visitors would feel equally at home, in a community of people selling things to other people who wanted to buy them. Twenty-thousand people showed up the first weekend to discover, as Eric puts it, "you can get quality things that are different from what you can get in Manhattan." This captures the Brooklyn spirit in a nutshell.

The Flea began with a handful of food vendors. Salvatore Ricotta (page 162) was the first food maker Eric pursued and persuaded to be part of the market, later to be joined by Whimsy & Spice (page 188), Nunu Chocolates (page 126), and Kumquat Cupcakery, now reinvented as Butter and Scotch (page 46). All were eager to participate in the Flea's maiden voyage. As the popularity of the market grew, so did the number of artisanal makers vying for a 10-foot by 10-foot booth and a chance to peddle their handcrafted wares to a hungry audience.

That success led to the expansion of the Flea to a second venue and the establishment of Smorgasburg, both in an empty lot in Williamsburg, in 2011. With more than 90 vendors, many of which are featured in this book, Smorgasburg is without a doubt the most extensive and tastiest food market in the country—dare I say the world. Where else can you eat your way through a one-of-a-kind ramen burger, a bowl of authentic Puerto Rican mofongo, a multi-layered Mexican cemita sandwich, a super fresh Red Hook lobster roll, and a mouth-watering Asia Dog? Full yet? How about some Dough doughnuts, People's Pops, and a Good Batch ice cream sandwich? Described as "one of the greatest urban experiences in New York," by *The New York Times*, Smorgasburg is a foodie nirvana.

For the makers, acceptance into the Flea and Smorgasburg means instantly becoming part of a network of like-minded chocolatiers and picklers, granola makers and bakers, supporting one other and recognizing that "the more stars that break out from the scene, the better it is for everyone," says Eric. And it's a stamp of approval that validates your Brooklyn brand and becomes your calling card to larger retailers around the country and, in many cases, the world.

Eric and Jonathan's latest venture is Berg'n, an expansive, 9,000-square-foot beer hall and food court, housed in a former Studebaker service station, on a mostly industrial street in Crown Heights. The food is small-batch, from a handful of Smorgasburg's beloved vendors. Served up concession-style, locals and food pilgrims share communal tables to devour great food and drink craft beer. Berg'n is the next step in the development of the Brooklyn Made food scene. The timeless and accessible atmosphere celebrates the Brooklyn brand as it settles in to a new groove, more mature and primed for the next wave of authentically Brooklyn makers.

RED HOOK

Red Hook is a perfect microcosm of what's transpiring all over the borough of Brooklyn. You can visit a good number of outstanding Brooklyn makers with a short stroll, and discover firsthand how the charm, variety, and rugged urban beauty of this 19th-century industrial waterfront community attracted so many fantastic 21st-century innovators and creators.

Here you will find vortex winnowers and melting tanks where cacao pods are turned into chocolate bars; copper-pot stills where small-batch whiskey is being distilled; custom-made stainless steel tanks where grapes and wild yeasts are being fermented. Red Hook also has its own share of food trucks, small urban farming lots, and bakers making incomparable treats.

To soak in the sites and the scents, hop on the B61 bus from downtown Brooklyn and get off on Red Hook's main drag, Van Brunt Street. Or take the New York Water Taxi at Pier 11 in Lower Manhattan that drops you off at the Ikea store in Red Hook ($5 weekdays each way, free on weekends).

On weekends the following makers are open for visits, tours, and tastings. Some even offer classes: check their websites for details before you go.

1. RED HOOK WINERY

In nice weather, when the doors of the 19th-century pier are thrown open, you can watch tugs and ferries crossing the harbor, and taste samples from Brooklyn's only winery. Tastings, daily, start at $8 * Free tour (15 minutes) with any tasting 1 PM Saturday and Sunday ONLY * Barrel Tasting & Tour (30 minutes) $25. Call to reserve a spot.
Hours: Monday–Saturday 11 AM–5 PM;
Sunday 12 PM–5 PM.
Pier 41, 325A, 175-204 Van Dyke Street, 347-689-2432
redhookwinery.com.

2. STEVE'S AUTHENTIC KEY LIME PIES

In 2001, Steve Tarpin was the first maker to move to Red Hook. His bakery shop was originally located at Pier 41, but after Hurricane Sandy he moved to higher ground at Pier 40. You can pop in and buy your key lime pie directly, when they're open.
Hours: Friday 11 AM–5 PM;
Saturday–Sunday 11 AM–sundown.
Pier 40, 185 Van Dyke Street,
718-858-5333
stevesauthentic.com.

3. CACAO PRIETO & WIDOW JANE

Visitors can buy from a shop set up between a still and the chocolate machines.
Hours: Please call for public hours.
218 Conover Street (Coffey Street),
347-225-0130
cacaoprieto.com

4. DRY DOCK WINE AND SPIRITS

A great liquor store where you can sample wares from Red Hook makers: Vermouth made by Uncouth Vermouth, and Sorel liqueur made by Jack From Brooklyn.
Hours: Monday–Thursday 12 PM–9 PM;
Friday–Saturday 10 AM–10 PM;
Sunday 12 PM–8 PM.
424 Van Brunt Street, 718-852-3625
drydockny.com

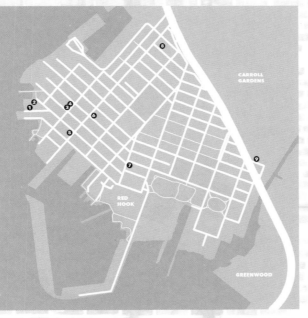

5. BAKED

This beautiful diner-style bakery offers chocolate chip cookies, cupcakes, three-layered cakes, and their classic dark brownies sprinkled with salt, all baked fresh daily.
Hours: Monday–Friday 7 AM–7 PM;
Saturday–Sunday 8 AM–7 PM
359 Van Brunt Street, 718-222-0345
bakednyc.com

6. VAN BRUNT STILLHOUSE

This distillery offers tours and has an active tasting room. Tours are $10/person (adults only please) and may be booked in advance online.
Tasting room hours:
Saturday–Sunday 1 PM–6 PM
6 Bay Street, 718-852-6405
vanbruntstillhouse.com

7. RAAKA

Taste raw cacao from different regions across the world, and see how it is transformed into smooth chocolate bars at Raaka's brand-new factory. The tour ends with a taste of all their signature craft bars. They offer 45-minute tours for $10 (min 4 people, max 16). Or take a class for $50 (min 4 people, max 12) and learn how to turn raw beans into bars. After a tour of the factory, you'll get to load Raaka's stone grinders with raw ingredients and pour your own bars into molds. At the end of the class, you'll have a bespoke, hand-crafted bar. Book a tour or class in advance on their website.
Tours: Tuesdays at 5 PM, Thursdays at 7 PM, Saturdays at 12 PM
Classes: Saturdays 2 PM–4 PM
64 Seabring Street, 855-255-3354
raakachocolate.com

8. OTHER HALF BREWING

Where Red Hook meets Carroll Gardens you will find Brooklyn's newest small-batch brewery and a cozy tasting room.
Hours: Thursday–Friday 5 PM–10 PM; Saturday–Sunday 12 PM–10 PM
195 Centre Street, 347-987-3527
otherhalfbrewing.com

BY BROOKLYN

To purchase many of the Brooklyn-made foods and beverages that we feature in our book visit Gaia DiLoreto's Smith Street gift shop, By Brooklyn (or her newly opened location in Williamsburg). Founded in 2011, By Brooklyn sells only products that are 100% manufactured in Brooklyn.

Having left behind a career in the finance industry and with a fresh degree from the Culinary Institute in her hands, Gaia was intrigued by the new artisans movement in Brooklyn, and committed herself to promoting Brooklyn food makers. She soon realized that Brooklyn artisans were producing more than just food products, and the idea for her store was born. Her cute storefront now carries a wide variety of Brooklyn-made products from clothes, totes, soaps, and glassware to specialty foods.

In addition to promoting Brooklyn makers in her shop, Gaia also serves on the Brooklyn Made Advisory Board. Sponsored by the Brooklyn Chamber of Commerce under the helm of Carlo A. Scissura, Brooklyn Made is the only certification program for goods made in Brooklyn. In order to get this sought-after designation, businesses must undergo a multi-faceted process to determine that they are authentically making their products in Brooklyn, as opposed to opportunistically borrowing the borough's cachet for branding purposes.

Scissura also created the Brooklyn Made Awards to celebrate the best of Brooklyn. To find out more check out: brooklynmade.nyc.

Gaia is a very strong promoter of the Brooklyn Made stamp of approval and its recognition of the efforts of Brooklyn Makers to keep manufacturing and job creation in Brooklyn despite obstacles such as high rents and a shortage of suitable spaces.

When we asked her for her favorite story about Brooklyn makers, Gaia told us about two very different makers that stand out equally in their commitment to the borough.

At Salty Road (page 160), Marisa Wu started hand-pulling taffy in Brooklyn, but when demand increased, she outsourced to locations in Massachusetts and Maine. In 2014, however, she decided to bring her taffy-making back to Brooklyn as she felt she was compromising the integrity of her product. With the help of a successful Kickstarter campaign, she raised enough money to be able to be make taffy in Brooklyn again.

Brooklyn Brine (page 32) is a success story for maker Shamus Jones, who started off in a small kitchen that he sublet in the overnight hours. Now he has built his own small factory in the Gowanus area and is running a $1 million-a-year pickling business. Brooklyn Brine also has international distribution, and recently shipped some 13,000 jars to retailers in South Africa and Japan. In choosing Brooklyn Brine as a representative of the best of Brooklyn, Gaia stresses Shamus' commitment to the quality of the product, his choice to employ local workers, and the fact that he chose deliberately to keep manufacturing in Brooklyn.

BY
BROOKLYN
Fine Goods
MADE in BROOKLYN, NY
CANARSIE
GRAVESEND
BUSHWICK
South Brooklyn

WHERE TO BUY

Here is a list of our favorite stores where you can buy Brooklyn-made food and beverages. We tossed in a few outdoor markets to explore new food makers, and a handful of online stores who are committed to carrying a wide range of Brooklyn products.

Bedford Cheese Shop
67 Irving Place, Gramercy, New York
229 Bedford Ave, Bedford, Brooklyn
BEDFORDCHEESESHOP.COM

Bklyn Larder
228 Flatbush Avenue, Prospect Heights, Brooklyn
WWW.BKLYNLARDER.COM

Blue Apron Foods
814 Union Street, Park Slope, Brooklyn
BLUE-APRON-FOODS.COM

Brooklyn Kitchen
100 Frost Street, Williamsburg, Brooklyn
THEBROOKLYNKITCHEN.COM

Brooklyn Victory Garden
920 Fulton Street, Clinton Hill, Brooklyn
BROOKLYNVICTORYGARDEN.COM

By Brooklyn
142 Grand Street, Williamsburg, Brooklyn
261 Smith Street, Carroll Gardens, Brooklyn
BYBROOKLYN.COM

Campbell Cheese Company
502 Lorimer Street, Williamsburg, Brooklyn
CAMPBELLCHEESE.COM

Court Street Grocers
485 Court Street, Carroll Gardens, Brooklyn
COURTSTREETGROCERS.COM

Dean & DeLuca
560 Broadway, New York
DEANDELUCA.COM

Depanneur
242 Wythe Avenue, Williamsburg, Brooklyn
DEPANNEURBKLYN.COM

Eastern District
1053 Manhattan Avenue, Greenpoint, Brooklyn
EASTERNDISTRICTNY.COM

Fairway Market
Various locations in New York City and Long Island
FAIRWAYMARKET.COM

Foragers
56 Adams Street, Dumbo, Brooklyn, and
233 Eighth Avenue, Chelsea, New York
FORAGERSMARKET.COM

Greene Grape Provisions
767 Fulton Street, Fort Greene, Brooklyn
GREENGRAPE.COM

Marlow & Daughters
95 Broadway, Williamsburg, Brooklyn
MARLOWANDDAUGHTERS.COM

Owl and Thistle General Store
833 Franklin Avenue, Crown Heights, Brooklyn
OWLANDTHISTLEGENERAL.COM

Park Slope Food Coop
782 Union Street, Park Slope, Brooklyn
FOODCOOP.COM

Stinky Bklyn
215 Smith Street, Carroll Gardens, Brooklyn
STINKYBKLYN.COM

Union Market
Various locations in Brooklyn and Manhattan
UNIONMARKET.COM

Valley Shepherd Creamery
211 Seventh Avenue, Park Slope, Brooklyn
VALLEYSHEPHERD.COM

West Elm
Various locations in New York City and the U.S.
WESTELM.COM

Whole Foods
Various locations in New York City and the U.S.

MARKETS

Berg'n:
899 Bergen Street, Crown Heights, Brooklyn
BERGN.COM
In 2014 the founders of Brooklyn Flea and Smorgasburg opened Berg'n, a beer hall and food court featuring locally-made beer and spirits, as well as a few Brooklyn food makers such as Parlor Cafe, Dough donuts, and Blue Marble Ice Cream.

Brooklyn Flea:
Founded in 2008, and now NYC's prime flea market with over 100 flea vendors and 30 food vendors, from April through November, this flea market takes place outdoors on Saturdays in Fort Greene and on Sundays in Williamsburg. For more details and updates on winter locations check: BROOKLYNFLEA.COM.

Smorgasburg:
A giant all-food market showcasing the best of Brooklyn's artisanal food scene, with 100 local and regional vendors in a beautiful waterfront setting. From April through November, this food market takes place each Saturday in Williamsburg at the East River State Park, and each Sunday at Brooklyn Bridge Park, Pier 5. For more details and updates on winter locations check: SMORGASBURG.COM.

WINE & LIQUOR

Bottle Shoppe
301 Bedford Avenue, Williamsburg, Brooklyn
353 Graham Avenue, Williamsburg, Brooklyn
THE BOOTLESHOPPENY.COM

Brooklyn Wine Exchange
138 Court Street, Cobble Hill, Brooklyn
BROOKLYNWINEEXCHANGE.COM

Dry Dock
424 Van Brunt Street, Red Hook, Brooklyn
DRYDOCKNY.COM

Gnarly Vines Wine & Spirits
350 Myrtle Ave, Fort Greene, Brooklyn
GNARLYVINES.COM

Gowanus Wine Merchants
493 Third Avenue, Gowanus, Brooklyn
GOWANUSWINES.COM

Michael Towne Wines & Spirits
73 Clark Street, Brooklyn Heights, Brooklyn
MICHAELTOWNEWINES.COM

Windsor Wine Merchants
216 Prospect Park West, Windsor Terrace, Brooklyn
WINDSORWINEMERCHANTS.COM

ONLINE STORES

ASTORWINES.COM
CHELSEAWINEVAULT.COM
FOOD52.COM
GOODEGGS.COM
HATCHERY.CO
MADECLOSE.COM
MOUTH.COM
WITHLOVEFROMBROOKLYN.COM

The Brooklyn food and drink scene is so active and bustling there was no way to feature all of our favorite makers. We want to acknowledge a few more here.

Baked in Brooklyn
Breuckelen Distilling
Brewla
Brooklyn Beet Company
Brooklyn Seltzer Boys
Bruce Cost Ginger Ale
D'Amico
Dona Chai
Fleisher's
Four & Twenty Blackbirds
Gustavo's Salsa
Hay Rosie
Kelso Beer
Manhattan Special
Nobletree
Parlor Coffee
Steve and Andy's
Stone Street Coffee Company
Tower Isle Patties

MAKERS' RETAIL BY NEIGHBORHOOD

Gotham Greens (p. 76)
810 Humboldt Street, 11222
gothamgreens.com

New York Distilling Company
(p. 122)
79 Richardson Street, 11211
nydistilling.com

Ovenly (p. 136)
31 Greenpoint Avenue, 11222
oven.ly

Pie Corps (p. 195)
77 Driggs Avenue, 11222
piecorps.com

PARK SLOPE

Bagel Hole (p. 18)
400 7th Avenue, 11215
bagelhole.net

Bark Hot Dogs (p. 193)
474 Bergen Street, 11217
barkhotdogs.com

Café Grumpy (p. 50)
383 7th Avenue, 11215
cafegrumpy.com

Colson Patisserie (p. 54)
374 9th Street, 11215
colsonpastries.com

Gorilla Coffee (p. 74)
97 5th Avenue, 11217
472 Bergen Street, 11217
gorillacoffee.com

Nunu Chocolates (p. 126)
179 Fifth Avenue, 11217
nunuchocolates.com

People's Pops (p. 142)
808 Union Street, 11215
peoplespop.com

PROSPECT HEIGHTS

Ample Hills Creamery (p. 12)
623 Vanderbilt Avenue, 11238
amplehills.com

Blue Marble (p. 28)
186 Underhill Avenue, 11238
bluemarbleicecream.com

Empire Mayonnaise Co.
(p. 193)
564 Vanderbilt Avenue, 11238
empiremayo.com

RED HOOK

BAKED (p. 20)
359 Van Brunt Street, 11231
bakednyc.com

Cacao Prieto (p. 48)
218 Conover Street, 11231
cacaoprieto.com

La Newyorkina (p. 108)
61 Commerce Street, 11231
lanewyorkina.com

Raaka (p. 195)
64 Seabring Street, 11231
raakachocolates.com

Red Hook Winery (p. 150)
Pier 41, 325 A, 175-204 Van
Dyke Street, 11231
redhookwinery.com

Van Brunt Stillhouse (p. 184)
6 Bay Street, 11231
vanbruntstillhouse.com

Widow Jane (p. 190)
218 Conover Street, 11231
widowjane.com

SHEEPSHEAD BAY

Jomart Chocolates (p. 94)
2917 Avenue R, 11229
jomartchocolates.com

Michael's of Brooklyn (p. 193)
2929 Avenue R, 11229
michaelsofbrooklyn.com

SUNSET PARK

Colson Patisserie (p. 54)
220 36th Street, 1st Floor, 11232
colsonpastries.com

Liddabit Sweets (p. 110)
220 36th St. 1st Floor, 11232
liddabitsweets.com

WILLIAMSBURG

Brooklyn Brewery (p. 30)
79 N 11th Street, 11249
brooklynbrewery.com

Brooklyn Cupcake (p. 34)
335 Union Avenue, 11211
brooklyncupcake.com

Mast Brothers (p. 114)
105 N 3rd Street, 11211
mastbrothers.com

Oslo Coffee Roasters (p. 132)
133 Roebling Street, 11211
328 Bedford Avenue, 11249
oslocoffee.com

* Check websites for
open hours

INDEX

BY PRODUCT

ACKNOWLEDGMENTS

First and foremost, thanks to everyone at powerHouse, especially Sharyn Rosart and Krzysztof Poluchowicz, for your editorial guidance and spot-on design, and Will Luckman for expert proofing and copyediting guidance. We couldn't have done it without you.

Thank you to *Edible Brooklyn* and particularly to Rachel Wharton and Gabrielle Langholtz, whose portraits of Brooklyn food and drink makers inspired us to write this book.

To Gaia DiLoreto at By Brooklyn, thank you for sharing your vast knowledge of the Brooklyn makers community. Your insight was invaluable and inspired us to look in every nook and cranny of this fine borough for delicious things to eat and drink.

Thanks to Kyle Devine from Brooklyn Wine Exchange for leading us towards a stream of libations and Susanne Kongoy from GRDN for hosting more than a few on-the-fly still-life photo sessions.

And to all the talented and inspiring Brooklyn makers, thanks for opening your doors and sharing your stories. We're in awe of you.

FROM SUSANNE: A tremendous thank you to my co-author Melissa, and to photographer Heather—I feel so lucky to have found you—without your enthusiasm, knowledge, and dedication to this crazy idea, this book would never have made it to publication.

Thank you to my dear friends and thanks especially to all of my colleagues at powerHouse who bore with me through the long process of researching and writing this book.

And a huge thank you goes to Daniel, for always giving me room to live my professional and private dreams: and to Louis, for being the best trouper and friend. I got a kick out of you guys tasting all those spicy condiments that I brought home. Are you ready for book #2?

Lastly, huge gratitude to my parents, who encouraged me to discover the world and its opportunities rather then stay in my comfortable high-school town—thanks to your support, I arrived in Brooklyn, my favorite place in the world, and the one that I now call home.

FROM MELISSA: Roan and Dory, thanks for always being so proud of me. I promise to keep the goodies coming! Love you two to bits.

Mom and Dad, thanks for your immeasurable support.

Jen, thanks for always checking in and keeping me looking ahead.

My dear friends, too many of you to name, thanks for your enthusiasm and encouragement; it means the world to me.

FROM HEATHER: Thank you to my team at home, Peter and Errolyn, who support me every day and never tire of yummy Brooklyn goods.

Photo © Heather Weston

SUSANNE KÖNIG is the director of and buyer for The POWERHOUSE Arena in Dumbo, Brooklyn, renowned for hosting eclectic cookbook parties for many Brooklyn-based chefs and makers including Pok Pok, Fleischer's, Kings County, Ample Hills, Sunday Suppers, franny's, BAKED, and many more. She also curates an extensive collection of Brooklyn-made products.

After spending her childhood and formative years in Germany, Belgium, and Paris where she worked at Sotheby's and for French art book publishers, she moved to New York in 2000. She works and lives in Brooklyn with her husband and son.

Photo © Daniel Paterna

MELISSA SCHREIBER VAUGHAN is the co-author of *The New Brooklyn Cookbook* and a recipe developer and tester, whose work has appeared in national food magazines and more than 20 cookbooks. Melissa curates food events throughout Brooklyn and lives in Park Slope with her two budding foodies, Roan and Dory. Check her out at: mrvcooks.wordpress.com.

Photo © Errolyn Daley

HEATHER WESTON takes pictures. Whether in the studio or on location she loves to photograph people and food. Heather lives in Brooklyn with her husband and daughter and is a proud ballet mom. To see more of her photography visit: www.heatherweston.com.

RACHEL WHARTON is a James Beard Foundation award-winning food writer, cookbook author, and contributing editor at *Edible Brooklyn*.

DAVID WONDRICH is one of the world's foremost American cocktail historians, a James Beard Foundation award-winning drinks writer, and the author of several books, including *Imbibe!*